698

OUR BILL OF RIGHTS:

WHAT IT MEANS TO ME

OUR BILL OF RIGHTS:

WHAT IT MEANS TO ME

A NATIONAL SYMPOSIUM

Edited by

JAMES WATERMAN WISE

Issued by

BILL OF RIGHTS SESQUI-CENTENNIAL COMMITTEE

LINCOLN BUILDING, NEW YORK

1941

329
W75 2

BILL OF RIGHTS
SESQUI-CENTENNIAL COMMITTEE

Honorary Chairman

FRANKLIN DELANO ROOSEVELT

Honorary Vice-Chairmen

JAMES M. COX

JOHN W. DAVIS

HERBERT HOOVER

CHARLES EVANS HUGHES

ALFRED M. LANDON

SAM RAYBURN

ALFRED E. SMITH

HENRY A. WALLACE

WENDELL WILLKIE

National Chairman

HERBERT BAYARD SWOPE

NATIONAL COMMITTEE

Helen C. White, *President*, AMERICAN ASSOCIATION OF UNIVERSITY WOMEN

Bess Duncan Wells, *National President*, AMERICAN GOLD STAR MOTHERS

Milo J. Warner, *Past National Commander*, THE AMERICAN LEGION

Mrs. Irving Fairweather, *National President*, AMERICAN WAR MOTHERS

Walter W. Head, *President*, BOY SCOUTS OF AMERICA

Lester F. Scott, *National Executive*, CAMP FIRE GIRLS

Mary C. Duffy, *Supreme Regent*, CATHOLIC DAUGHTERS OF AMERICA

Joseph Berning, *Supreme President*, THE CATHOLIC KNIGHTS OF AMERICA

Raymond Gram Swing, *Chairman*, COUNCIL FOR DEMOCRACY

LAURENCE R. MELTON, *National Commander*, DISABLED AMERICAN VETERANS OF THE WORLD WAR.

Samuel McCrea Cavert, *General Secretary*, THE FEDERAL COUNCIL OF THE CHURCHES OF CHRIST IN AMERICA

John S. McClelland, *Grand Exalted Ruler*, GRAND LODGE, BENEVOLENT AND PROTECTIVE ORDER OF ELKS

Fred S. Harris, *National Commander*, JEWISH WAR VETERANS OF THE UNITED STATES

Francis P. Matthews, *Supreme Knight*, KNIGHTS OF COLUMBUS

Charles H. Johnson, *Grand Secretary*, GRAND LODGE FREE AND ACCEPTED MASONS, NEW YORK STATE

James J. Davis, *Director General*, LOYAL ORDER OF MOOSE

Walter White, *Secretary*, NATIONAL ASSOCIATION FOR THE ADVANCEMENT OF COLORED PEOPLE

Mrs. Maurice L. Goldman, *President*, NATIONAL COUNCIL OF JEWISH WOMEN

Myrtle Hooper Dahl, *President*, NATIONAL EDUCATION ASSOCIATION OF THE UNITED STATES

Joe Hanley, *Commander-in-Chief*, UNITED SPANISH WAR VETERANS

J. Louis Reynolds, *President General*, UNITED STATES FLAG ASSOCIATION

Robert B. Handy, Jr., *Adjutant General*, VETERANS OF FOREIGN WARS OF THE UNITED STATES

Eugene Barnett, *General Secretary, National Council*, YOUNG MEN'S CHRISTIAN ASSOCIATION

Frederick M. Warburg, *President*, YOUNG MEN'S HEBREW ASSOCIATION

Mrs. Henry A. Ingraham, *President, National Board*, YOUNG WOMEN'S CHRISTIAN ASSOCIATIONS

Mrs. Ray F. Schwartz, *Executive Director*, YOUNG WOMEN'S HEBREW ASSOCIATION

TABLE OF CONTENTS

TABLE OF CONTENTS

FOREWORD

Things of the spirit never die. They flame anew each time they are under fire. They are flaming high at this moment.

Bombs may blow the body to bits, but they bind the soul together.

This book is testimony to the spirit of man; to his personality; to his right to be decent.

From the beginning of time men have had to fight for this sort of life. The fight has never been easy, but it has always been won.

As long as men believe in Freedom they will achieve it. The Dark Ages shall not return.

When Freedom dies man lives on his knees. When Freedom lives man walks erect.

The Bill of Rights is our Prayer Book and our promise of salvation. The cause of Freedom is the cause of God. That is the dedication of this volume.

None of us is wise enough to say finally what one event is the greatest in our history. There are some that cry aloud for that description:

The Declaration of Independence; the Treaty of Paris, ending the Revolutionary War; the adoption

of the Constitution; the pronouncement of the
Monroe Doctrine; the Emancipation Proclamation;
the end of the War between the States; the war for
Freedom and Democracy, begun in 1917—and still
going on.

I have left to the last, although it belongs at the
top, the formulation and adoption of the Bill of Rights
—the first ten amendments to the Constitution, adopted
by the baby nation December 15, 1791.

In this group of principles are to be found the soul
and spirit of the Constitution. With the Bill of Rights
added, the Constitution becomes nearly a perfect
thing. Without the Bill, the seven articles of the original draft are largely given over to the protection of
property.

Jefferson, shocked by the omissions in the Constitution, as promulgated in 1789, while he was United
States Minister to France (another type of France
than Vichy represents today!) drafted the additions
to our great charter. Thus we were given the Four
Freedoms by which we grew strong in self-reliance;
in courage; in independence and in self-respect.

The Amendments gave us Free Speech; Free Press;
Free Worship; Free Assembly and also the right to
petition. They gave us full protection of the citizen
against oppression; the right of trial by jury and,
generally, the right of the individual against the state.
Jefferson said himself, speaking in the prophetic tone
that is true of great men:

"The Bill of Rights is what the people are entitled

to against every government."

This publication is testimony to an immortal writing that will live with the Ten Commandments; the Sermon on the Mount; Magna Charta and those other great fountains of faith by which men live.

Today we fight again for the ideals that democracy gives to us as rights. We shall never lose them; the whole world some day will achieve them.

To help all of us to realize the high privilege we have of living under the Bill of Rights, the thoughts contained herein were put in words by men and women who believe the fires of Freedom must always burn brightly and sometimes fiercely. Now is one of those times.

—HERBERT BAYARD SWOPE, *Chairman*,
   Bill of Rights Sesqui-Centennial Committee

Bill Of Rights

The first ten amendments to the Constitution, known as "A Bill of Rights," were adopted by the first Congress, called to meet in New York City, March 4, 1789. They were later ratified by the various States, and on December 15, 1791, were made a part of the Constitution.

AMENDMENT I
Freedom of Religion, Speech, and the Press; Right of Assembly and Petition

CONGRESS SHALL MAKE no law respecting an establishment of religion, or prohibiting the free exercise thereof; or abridging the freedom of speech, or of the press, or the right of the people peaceably to assemble, and to petition the government for a redress of grievances.

AMENDMENT II
Right to Keep and Bear Arms

A well regulated militia, being necessary to the security of a free state, the right of the people to keep and bear arms shall not be infringed.

AMENDMENT III
Quartering of Soldiers

No soldier shall in time of peace be quartered in any house without the consent of the owner, nor in time of war, but in a manner to be prescribed by law.

Amendment IV
Regulation of Right of Search and Seizure

The right of the people to be secure in their persons, houses, papers, and effects, against unreasonable searches and seizures, shall not be violated, and no warrants shall issue but upon probable cause, supported by oath or affirmation, and particularly describing the place to be searched and the person or things to be seized.

Amendment V
Protection for Persons and Their Property

No person shall be held to answer for a capital or otherwise infamous crime, unless on a presentment or indictment of a grand jury, except in cases arising in the land or naval forces, or in the militia, when in actual service in time of war or public danger; nor shall any person be subject for the same offense to be twice put in jeopardy of life or limb; nor shall be compelled in any criminal case to be a witness against himself, nor be deprived of life, liberty, or property, without due process of law; nor shall private property be taken for public use, without just compensation.

Amendment VI
Rights of Persons Accused of Crime

In all criminal prosecutions, the accused shall enjoy the right to a speedy and public trial by an impartial jury of the State and district wherein the crime shall have been committed, which district shall have been previously ascertained by law, and to be informed of the nature and cause of the accusation; to be confronted with the witnesses against him; to have compulsory process for obtaining witnesses in his favor, and to have the assistance of counsel for his defense.

Amendment VII
Right of Trial by Jury in Suits at Common Law

In suits at common law, where the value in controversy shall exceed twenty dollars, the right of trial by jury shall be preserved, and no fact tried by a jury shall be otherwise re-examined in any court of the United States, than according to the rules of the common law.

Amendment VIII
Protection Against Excessive Bail and Punishments

Excessive bail shall not be required, nor excessive fines imposed, nor cruel and unusual punishments inflicted.

Amendment IX
Constitution Does Not List All Individual Rights

The enumeration in the Constitution of certain rights shall not be construed to deny or disparage others retained by the people.

Amendment X
Powers Reserved to the States and the People

The powers not delegated to the United States by the Constitution, nor prohibited by it to the States, are reserved to the States respectively, or to the people.

The Four Freedoms

AS THE SECOND YEAR of world conflict comes to an end America is face to face with certain grim realities. It is apparent that the expense attached to the defense effort will run into an appalling sum. The sweeping readjustments that will eventually reach every family are becoming clearer by the day. The need for redirection of our whole economy in order to supply plants which manufacture implements of war with an abundance of raw materials is now painfully obvious.

Yes, the world that we know is being refashioned. But so be it, and although the disappearance of familiar patterns and habits of living brings a momentary shock, there must be no regrets, no longing backward glances. Neither can we afford to hang our heads, wring our hands and insist that we cannot defend democracy without destroying it. After all the only disaster that will overtake us is the disaster that comes from indecision and inaction.

Nevertheless, as we throw all our material resources into the struggle against the forces of aggression we must also seek to retain the virtues of more peaceful living. Just as the person in deadly peril seizes upon a cherished object to protect, come what may, we must fix upon our precepts of democratic government and preserve them no matter what the cost.

There are a good many of these precepts, but I have in mind several in particular. I am thinking of how the American—man or woman, rich or poor—can walk down the avenue unafraid that a heavy hand is going to drop on his shoulder. I am thinking of how the American—no matter what his calling, his background—can talk, and believe, and worship as he sees fit without fear of reprisals for non-conformity. I am thinking of the personal liberty guaranteed every citizen of this country in the Bill of Rights of the Constitution.

I like to remind myself of the origin of the Bill of Rights. It came into being at a time of great distress and clearly represented the desires of a people who had paid a high price for their independence and were determined to keep it. Since that time it has weathered an internal conflict, foreign wars, periods of economic depression. Even during these emergencies there has been no foreshortening of the scope of the Bill of Rights, nor has its fundamental character been altered. Invariably after these crises have passed each American has turned his face homeward and found to his intense joy his personal liberty inviolate.

This augurs well for the future. Perhaps the destructive forces loose in the world will assume more awesome proportions than any yet seen; perhaps the dangers and hardships of the civilian population will be greater than ever before; but I cannot believe that these new developments will serve to swerve us from our course any more than the vicissitudes of the past.

Undoubtedly it will mean a vigilant citizenry constantly on guard. But we have that. Undoubtedly it will mean leadership of the highest quality. But we have that, too. In fact, I can think of no more impressive reiteration of belief in the Bill of Rights than that made by Franklin D. Roosevelt in his message to Congress last January:

"In the future days which we seek to make secure, we look forward to a world founded upon four essential human freedoms.

"The first is freedom of speech and expression—everywhere in the world.

"The second is freedom of every person to worship God in his own way—everywhere in the world.

"The third is freedom from want . . .

"The fourth is freedom from fear . . .

"That is no vision of a distant millennium. It is a definite basis for a kind of world attainable in our own time and generation. That kind of world is the very antithesis of the so-called 'new order' of tyranny which the dictators seek to create with the crash of a bomb.

"This nation has placed its destiny in the hands, heads and hearts of its millions of free men and women, and its faith in freedom under the guidance of God. Freedom means the supremacy of human rights everywhere. Our support goes to those who struggle to gain those rights and keep them. Our strength is our unity of purpose.

"To that high concept there can be no end save victory."

—MARY ANDERSON,
Director, Women's Bureau,
United States Department of Labor

Religion And The Bill Of Rights

WE ACCEPT OUR LIBERTY, as we do our health, pretty much as a matter of course, hardly giving it a thought until we begin to lose it. Then we become conscious of how much it means.

Experience throughout the long period of human history teaches that liberty must be won in every generation and can be held only by "eternal vigilance." As foes of freedom the aggressors reappear with different weapons, but always with the same aim—to destroy the souls of freemen.

That religion and democracy are closely linked together is a truism proved amply in the history of our country. The American colonies were settled by men and women seeking a free life, as well as a home for freedom. Religion was written prominently into their agreements, covenants, pacts and constitutions, but the early colonists made no provision for the free exercise of religion. Those who had "fled before the demands of conformity" later determined by law that others must conform "or get out of the colony." It was said of Governor Endicott of the Massachusetts Bay Colony, "If he had found 'toleration' in his dictionary, he

19

would have cut the word out, just as he drew his sword and cut the red cross out of the English flag because it represented the ancient Catholic faith of England." This attitude, formulated into law and supported by stern preaching, led to the founding of Rhode Island by Roger Williams and his associates. They were the first ones to put into practice the principle of the independence of the individual conscience even beyond the grants of liberty by the state. Maryland was founded by a small company of Catholics seeking "freedom of worship" in 1634, only fourteen years after the Protestant Pilgrims had landed at Plymouth.

Under Lord Baltimore's liberal rule there developed a large degree of freedom in religion, as well as a remarkable advance in democratic procedure. The people of Maryland not only took part in making their laws but were given power to originate laws. No other colony at the time enjoyed quite as much freedom and in 1649 the Assembly passed the "Toleration Act" which confirmed by law these liberties. Following this action Maryland became the refuge not only for the oppressed Catholics from England, but Protestants from some of the other American colonies, Puritans from Virginia, Quakers and others who found congenial homes in this colony. It is true that the "Toleration Act" was not very broad in that it tolerated only those of the Christian religion, but it was a step forward on the road to liberty and marked a greater advance than anything even in England at the time. It remained for the colony at Providence, Rhode Island to advance the Act of Toleration by granting full religious freedom to Christians and Jews and even to those without any religious affiliation or belief. The Act affirmed "that men of all religions, and men of no religion, should live unmolested so long as they behaved themselves."

The Bill of Rights was fashioned and adopted as a part of the Constitution of the United States of America as a guarantee against the dangers of enslavement by the majority, for which the Constitution provides and upon which it confers such wide powers. Experience under the British Parliamentary system had proven that Parliament was almost omnipotent. Blackstone said, "It can do everything that is not naturally impossible to be done." In other words, Parliament could not turn water into wine, or raise the dead—but there were no other limitations at that time!

The first ten Amendments put the essential rights of free men and women beyond the power of abolition or serious abridgement, even by the Congress they themselves had elected. The first of these rights is "freedom of worship." DeTocqueville in his study of "Democracy in America" came to the conclusion that the character of "Anglo-American civilization is the result of the incorporated and combined spirit of religion and the spirit of liberty." Further he says, "Religion is no less the companion of liberty in all its battles and its triumphs; the cradle of its infancy and the divine source of its claims. The safeguard of morality is religion, and morality is the best security of law and the surest pledge of freedom."

Since the days when this distinguished Frenchman visited us our nation has expanded more than ten times in population and has become fabulously rich in resources. The dangers today are different in form and are multiplied in horror, but the fundamental issues are the same. The results of research have made possible our great technological advance. Communications are easy and reach to the ends of the earth. But is our progress really progress? If so, then what is our destiny? Our chief danger is that which has faced all free men:—the danger that the lesser good will blind us to the greater good, and that we will lose through sloth and incomprehension what has been gained and held at so great a cost—our liberty.

Unity in purpose, in thought and in action was never more essential but this unity does not mean uniformity. In fact, the very attempt to force uniformity will make impossible true unity. The papers published in the "Federalist", written by Hamilton, Madison and Jay for "the purpose of commending to the acceptance of the people of the thirteen Colonies the Constitution tendered them by the Federal Convention," reveal a unity with considerable difference of opinion. For instance, Hamilton was opposed to making any amendments to the Constitution and was almost bitter in his attack on the Bill of Rights. He argued that in the Preamble to the Constitution everything is said that needs to be said as a recognition of popular rights

—"We, the people of the United States, to secure the blessings of liberty to ourselves and our posterity, do ordain and establish this Constitution." He then characterizes the ten proposed Amendments as "aphorisms which would sound much better in a treatise of ethics than in a Constitution of government."

The Bill of Rights was adopted, and now a Hundred and Fifty Years after its ratification it still stands as the charter of our liberties.

We, with free people everywhere, are menaced by the war which now engulfs four-fifths of the people of the whole world. Never has there been a more brutal onslaught and the spearhead of this aggression is thrust at the heart of democracy—our Bill of Rights. The future of our own and all democratic government hangs in the balance. Blood is being shed as never before.

This is our world and our fight. If aggression wins in Europe, we all will soon learn that Hitler's world has moved a long way toward realization. Hitler was right when he said: "These two worlds (his and the democratic) cannot live together; they must break apart."

We celebrate the ratification of the Bill of Rights in a dark period. We may continue to disagree on minor things but the risk is too great for us to remain oblivious to the dangers we face. There are some objectors and dissidents, many of them honest in their convictions, but blind to what is actually happening. The vast majority of our people know what we face and accept the inevitable with hope and courage. Our nation is rising to the occasion.

We pledge our allegiance to and renew our faith in our way of life; faith in that Providence which we believe has led us all these years, and faith in ourselves to be strong enough to unite us in these bitter hours of decision. Madison said of the Constitution: "Had no important step been taken by the leaders of the Revolution for which a precedent could not be discovered . . . the people of the United States might at this moment have been numbered among the melancholy victims of misguided counsels; might at best have been laboring under the weight of some of those forms (of oppression) which have crushed the liberties of the rest of mankind. Happily for America, happily for the whole human race, they pursued a new and more noble course."

—HENRY A. ATKINSON,
  General Secretary, The Church Peace Union

Guard The Ramparts

IT IS OF FIRST importance that the study of the Constitution should be an essential part not only of the
education of the American youth, but of all Americans, and especially those who have become natural-
ized citizens of this great nation. While all of us
cannot be trained in the technicalities of the law, we
should all have some idea of our fundamental institutions. We need to know their relationship to our daily
life, the reasons for their existence, and the benefits
we derive from them, as well as the importance to
ourselves of their perpetuation. The Constitution is
not self-perpetuated by any means; if it is to survive
it will be because it has the support of the people—not
passive, but an active public support. This means making adequate sacrifice to maintain that which is of the
greatest benefit to the greatest number.

The Constitution has its roots in the great and
heroic past of the English speaking race. Today, under
that Constitution which was adopted through the
blood and sweat of the pioneers of our country, the
safeguard of personal liberty is ever present. Under
our great Bill of Rights, our governmental power is

divided into three parts. The first is the power granted to the central government; the second that reserved to the States, and the third and by far the most important, although at times the fact may not be generally recognized, the power reserved to the people under the many inhibitions of both State and Federal legislation.

In the turmoil which now seems to have engulfed the entire world, the citizens of the United States should well remember the last part particularly—it is the people, those who go to make up the great cross section of this country, who must guard the ramparts from the ever increasing dangers of Nazism, Fascism and Communism. Our Constitution is the final safeguard of every right that is enjoyed by any American citizen. As long as it is observed those rights will be secure, but should it fall into disrespect or disrepute the way of orderly, organized government as we have known it for the past one hundred and fifty years will be at an end.

Americans everywhere must stand guard.

—W. WARREN BARBOUR,
United States Senator

The Right To Freedom

WHEN THE FEDERAL CONSTITUTION was submitted on September 28, 1787, by Congress to the Legislatures of the several States for ratification there was very strong opposition in all the States to its adoption. The Democrats, under the leadership of Thomas Jefferson, feared that the provisions of the instrument would unduly abridge State's rights and result in a government too highly centralized for their views. It was necessary for nine States to ratify before the Constitution took effect. It was not until June 21, 1788, that the ninth State, New Hampshire, gave its approval. The States, which had not ratified up to that time, were Virginia, New York, North Carolina and Rhode Island. Virginia and New York gave their assent in 1788. When President Washington was inaugurated on April 30, 1789 on the steps of the Federal Hall in New York, neither North Carolina nor Rhode Island had ratified and, therefore, were not one of the United States. These two reluctant States did, however, come into line. North Carolina ratified on November 21, 1789, and Rhode Island on May 29, 1790.

It will be seen by this long delay how strong was the feeling against the Constitution. Undoubtedly it would never have been ratified had it not been for the assurance given by Congress and by the leaders who favored the Constitution, especially Alexander Hamilton and James Madison, that the Bill of Rights would be adopted as soon as the Constitution was ratified. This pledge was carried out and the first ten amendments to the Constitution, forming the Bill of Rights, were proposed to the Legislatures of the States on September 25, 1789 and were thereafter ratified. It will be seen how much importance our founding fathers attached to the Bill of Rights. Without undertaking to enumerate all the rights secured to the people by these ten amendments, there may be mentioned the rights of religious freedom, of freedom of speech and of the press, the right to assemble and to petition, the right to due process of law, and the right to trial by jury.

Assuredly there has never been a time in the history of the world when it was more necessary to lay emphasis on these great fundamental rights. While all intelligent persons realize that in times of great emergency the people must voluntarily consent to some suspension of these rights, nevertheless it should always be borne in mind that such suspension is merely temporary and for a specific occasion. Our Government is founded upon the right of its citizens to all reasonable freedom of every kind. It is this great right that is protected by the first ten Amendments to the Constitution known as the Bill of Rights.

—GEORGE GORDON BATTLE,
*Co-Chairman, Council Against
Intolerance in America*

Rights Carry Duties

THE BILL OF RIGHTS was a pacer in the democratic movement in America and as such is entitled to all the prestige of leadership. Yet it really took a century after its enactment for American women to procure the Nineteenth Amendment to the federal Constitution which compelled reluctant states to grant them the basic right of the free—the right to vote. Non-Christian men and freethinkers of their sex more readily wrested from state legislatures the guarantee of their civil rights. But it was not until Lincoln's Emancipation Proclamation and the passage of the Fifteenth Amendment that race ceased to be, by law, a barrier to the enjoyment of civil liberties for all American men. With the celebration in this year, 1941, of the original Bill of Rights should therefore be coupled the celebration of its enlarged guarantees.

But even the original Bill of Rights would have been a dead letter if dauntless men and women, risking death, had not taught the public to listen without rioting to opinions which it abhorred. That educational process enabled the letter of the law to live in practice, or application, for the American way of life. In celebrating the original Bill of Rights now, we should celebrate with it the courage and skill of the men and the women who made tolerance a fact as well as a principle of law. The open forum, so characteristic of American democracy, owes its inception and its continuation to persons of both sexes who insisted that law and practice were parts of the same thing.

That rights carry duties has become a third aspect of democratic evaluations, nurtured on free debates. It is increasingly understood in America that liberty could become license; that rights if viewed as extreme personal privileges could reduce society to anarchy. There is today, in connection with rights, the wide prevalence of the philosophy that rights are granted to individuals in order that they may develop their talents for competent voluntary cooperation in the thought and action essential to the strength of society, to general welfare, and to the very endurance of civil liberties themselves.

Theoretically, the tolerance provided for by rights might induce such lethargy of minds and morals on the part of the many that the willful few could gain social control and set up a totalitarian system of government. But history has produced effective revolts amid persecution—to become in turn tyrannies.

Accordingly, with the value assigned to rights and the tolerance they imply must be blended the ideas of statecraft, power, responsibility to the common life, and the good life for all—if rights and tolerance are to persist.

—MARY R. BEARD

The Strength Of Our Democracy

A HISTORY OF civilization could be written around the derivation of the privileges that constitute our Bill of Rights. The emphasis would be not on rulers and governments, but on the struggle mankind has waged for centuries to obtain recognition of the rights of individual men. These rights are guarantees necessary to any people who wish to live in the free atmosphere of liberty. They are the foundation of any government that exists by the free will of the governed and not by the military force of self-appointed rulers.

The history of our own Bill of Rights is fired with the determination of the American people to preserve their liberties as individuals living in a free state. It is significant that these first ten Amendments in our Constitution were drawn from earlier declarations of rights which a number of the original thirteen States had formulated for themselves before they joined the Union. They not only served as models for our Federal Constitution but became basic patterns for new democracies all over the world.

Today there is abroad in the world a monstrous force that would set the clock back and re-establish regimes that rank the state above the individual. Already in many lands fundamental rights have been destroyed; and the existence of our own is threatened. Such crises have occurred before in the history of man but never with such ruthless vehemence and on such a world-wide scale.

While it is fitting to commemorate this 150th Anniversary, let us not honor the Bill of Rights simply as an historical memory. It belongs not only to the past. It is indispensable to contemporary life; without its basic assumptions there is no future for America. We must not only protect its guarantees, we must devote ourselves to the aggressive use of the rights themselves. For it is in the vigorous exercise of those rights that the strength of our democracy lies. On their survival rests the hope of freedom throughout the world.

—Francis Biddle,
Attorney General of the United States

Soul Of Our Nation

THE BILL OF RIGHTS has for us a peculiar significance today when we are trying to make clear to ourselves those few profound principles which shape our nation in the form of what we call a democracy. The essential of democracy is not to be found in any statement of liberties or in any body of laws protecting rights, or even in any form of government. It is to be found only in provision for change and development. Any form fixed and forever may become the grave of democracy. But any form which remains forever provisional, which allows amendment and change, which grows as the will of the people grows toward freedom, is the safeguard of liberty.

In our Bill of Rights there is this safeguard. The Bill of Rights began with a protest, our protest against our own newly made Constitution, because there was not expressed clearly enough in it this possibility for change as we changed. Freedom is a living expanding thing. A child develops from helplessness into the complete freedom of the individual. So our nation when it began could not comprehend in one age the full meaning of freedom for all time ahead. But those first Americans knew that above all there must be room for change, and the group of amendments which we call the Bill of Rights was that room.

We Americans ought, therefore, to guard as the very soul of our nation this Bill of Rights, not only for what it already says but far more for what it may let other amendments say in the future. We ought to see to it as our primary duty that there is never an end put to this Bill of Rights. The Constitution must remain unfinished, ready for new articles, sensitive to our own change and growth toward a better democracy, a more complete freedom for all Americans alike.

I look forward to the day when not only in our Constitution but also in the laws of all our States can be found the principles which will give to colored Americans the same justice and freedom that white Americans now have, to that day when women shall have equal opportunity and responsibility with men, to that day when there need be no more fear and despair in the hearts of the poor, the aged, the handicapped. The hope of our democracy lies in our Bill of Rights.

—PEARL S. BUCK

Protection Of The Individual

FUNDAMENTALLY, THE BILL OF RIGHTS, as embodied in the Constitution of the United States, particularly in the first ten Amendments, is the recognition by the Government of the dignity of the individual, and a prohibition against any infringement on those rights, or that individual dignity, by Government itself.

The Bill of Rights, in other words, deals with the protection of the individual against his Government. The protection of an individual against another individual or group of individuals is not implicit in the Bill of Rights, but falls more into the realm of police powers of the Government.

Take the First Amendment. This provides that "Congress shall make no law" restricting freedom of religion, freedom of speech and press, nor the right of assemblage and petition. By implication we, as a people, have taken this to mean guarantee of freedom of religion, speech, and press, and the right of assemblage and petition, though I am not certain that the Supreme Court of the United States (as in the matter of Jehovah's Witnesses) always has supported this implication.

Other provisions of the Bill of Rights, to bear arms; freedom from quartering of troops; protection against unreasonable searches and seizures without proper warrant; habeas corpus; trial by jury; jury shall have sole determination of facts; prohibition against excessive bail—all these are for the protection of the individual against his Government.

Two other provisions of the Bill of Rights (1) failure to enumerate certain rights shall not deny or disparage those retained by the people, and (2) powers not delegated to the United States, nor prohibited to the States, are reserved to the States, or to the people, do not deal so directly with the rights of the individual.

So much for the legal angle, the "letter" of the Bill of Rights. Of as great moment in our world today, is the acceptance by all of us of the great principle embodied in the Bill of Rights—Tolerance. Intolerance by the people themselves can, and will, destroy the principle of the Bill of Rights—security of the dignity of the individual—almost entirely, even if there is strict observance of the letter of the Bill of Rights by Government.

We ourselves must live up to the fundamental principle of the Bill of Rights, or the Bill of Rights becomes a dead letter.

—ARTHUR CAPPER,
United States Senator

Our Strongest Guarantee

WHEN THE FIRST CONGRESS assembled in New York in 1791, its first act was to pass the Bill of Rights—as the first ten Amendments to our Constitution are popularly called. This Bill of Rights granted to all citizens freedom of speech, of religion, of assembly and of the press. It marked a magnificent advance in defense of liberty and has become our strongest guarantee against human slavery. It has given the poor man the same legal rights as the millionaire. The law of this land protects all alike. This Bill of Rights has preserved our country as "the land of the free" for the past one hundred and fifty years. Our highest duty is to conserve it to future generations. Its use must be protected; its abuse must be prevented.

In this generation, our Bill of Rights is suffering sharp attacks though many Americans either do not know or do not wish to know of the danger. Because it grants freedom of speech, foreign propagandists spread their false doctrines among our citizens. Because it upholds a free press, millions of Nazi articles and magazines condemning our American way—and some even published at government expense—are delivered into American homes by our government-paid letter carriers. Because it stands for religious freedom, many speakers use the platform and radio to breathe hatred against followers of other creeds.

The authors of this freedom-granting Bill of Rights never intended it to defeat the four freedoms their law champions. Its shocking abuse may lead to that end. Therefore, Americans must make sacrifices for the Bill of Rights. One sacrifice must be to surrender a fraction of freedom in order to save freedom.

Such a sacrifice in 1861 saved our country from disunion. When Civil War threatened our very existence, President Lincoln temporarily assumed dictatorial powers. In curtailing individual rights, he defended his action by saying "It is better to save the Union without a Constitution than to save the Constitution without a Union." Future events justified the President's course.

Today, as our nation faces another crisis, we should place sensible guards around our sacred Bill of Rights so that it will continue to serve Humanity and protect human freedom for another one hundred and fifty years.

—RUDOLPH I. COFFEE,
President, Temple of Religion,
San Francisco

Reciprocal Rights And
Responsibilities

LOOKING BACK over the 150 years of American history since our forefathers wrote the Bill of Rights into our national Constitution, we can be proud that each succeeding generation has guarded so intelligently the fundamental liberties those notable Amendments confirmed. Every proposed exception has been subjected to the microscope of public scrutiny, for the American people have been determined to maintain this heritage of freedom.

As life has become increasingly complex and our people more interdependent, limitations have necessarily increased. Yet those limitations have been jealously watched in order that they might not involve denial of the underlying rights.

But have we assumed, to the extent that this increase in the complexity and interdependence of our way of life has required, the responsibilities that attend all rights,—responsibilities that are essential to their preservation? I think not. Rather than exercise self-discipline and self-regulation, we have turned to government more and more, as if it were the sole means of checking abuses by individuals, the sole agency for

39

curbing the attempt of one group to benefit at the expense of another. That way lies the suicide of freedom.

We of business wish, for example, to maintain a wide field open for the enterprising of our people. History has taught, and the current experience of other nations confirms, the fact that all the liberties we cherish are inseparably bound up with this freedom for the exercise of initiative and ingenuity by individuals and by voluntary groups in enterprise. And in it we have found the road to an amazing rise in the standard of living and to an unparalleled spread of cultural as well as economic opportunity. Are we willing to abandon that right because we lack foresight and determination to use our freedom effectively?

The Machine Age, with its transformation of our economic activities, has raised problems that must be solved. The passing of the present emergency will intensify those problems. The question wage workers, managements, and investors must ask themselves, as individuals and as groups, seems to me clear. Will they have the wisdom to undertake, in voluntary consultation and co-operation, with such aid from government as may be needed, the resolving of the problems that concern them directly and the public welfare generally? Or will they resign themselves, with vain protests, to arbitrary action by government—a method surely less intelligent and less hopeful than one designed to reach solutions through the consensus of representatives of all interests concerned.

The American people, almost without exception, wish to make democracy work. The aim of organized society is the welfare of the men, women and children who compose it. Through pressure of public opinion our people can insist that democratic processes be applied to the solution of their problems. They can require self-discipline on the part of every economic interest—whether investors, producers on the farms, or management and labor in industry and trade—for this is nothing more than requiring it of themselves. They can demand the exercise of social responsibility by all groups as an essential to the maintenance of their rights.

This democratic procedure will involve continuous social adjustment. To be effective such adjustment must be reached by intelligent voluntary co-operation that anticipates critical situations, not by ill-considered arbitrary coercion that is extemporized to deal with such situations after they have developed.

In the long run we shall maintain our rights just about in proportion as we exercise our responsibilities.

—HOWARD COONLEY,
   Former President,
   National Association of Manufacturers

Validated In Blood

THE BODY AND BONE of American Democracy were created by the Constitution. The bloodstream was injected in 1791 with the first ten Amendments. Without these Amendments, assuring the rights of men, the American democracy would have been a soulless machine.

The Bill of Rights proclaims the sacredness of the human personality, and the determination to let it develop and express itself in a freedom bounded only by democratically enacted curbs against license. What its guarantees mean to individual men has often been imperfectly seen by persons complacent in the possession of them; but in lands beyond the seas we have been permitted to see clearly what is meant by the absence of them.

The Bill of Rights expresses a concept the triumph of which we never dare take for granted. It was inaugurated in blood and from time to time it has been validated in blood. Sometimes the sacrifice falls on the individual, a martyr to sternly held conviction. Sometimes it falls on a nation, as on that nation now whose people have pledged themselves to fight on the beaches, in the fields, in the streets rather than submit to a force which would deprive them of their sacred freedom.

Whenever the call is made, it must and will be answered; not only by a Patrick Henry shouting, "Give me liberty or give me death!" but by an Elijah Lovejoy, actually embracing death in the defense of his freedom to print; not only by a sailor sinking beneath the torpedo's foam, but by a sheriff defending his prisoner from a mob. The Bill of Rights must be defended with passion, not passivity.

To hew to this line is particularly hard in a time of world tumult. In such a time, in the name of "Liberty, Equality, Fraternity," a Robespierre sent his thousands to the guillotine. Our own land has known excesses of intolerance. It may know them again. As this is written, our lives and liberties are threatened from without by a great conflagration. In our own defense we are building a backfire. A moment's relaxation of our principles and we could be consumed by our own flame.

The day the Bill of Rights passes from public reverence, democracy is finished in America. That day falls the frontier on which sane men and women everywhere are already, in their dreams, building a better world.

—JAMES M. COX,
Ex-Governor of Ohio

A Sacred Stewardship

"IN ADDITION TO HOLDING firmly to our Bill of Rights, we should formulate a Bill of Duties." This insistence upon the stewardship of citizenship, urged during the summer by Vice-President Henry Wallace, in an address before the Foreign Policy Association, received significant response throughout the nation.

One New York State Editor, commented as follows: "In the totalitarian states citizens have duties but no rights. Under our democratic system some people have mistakenly assumed that they have rights but no duties." Perhaps there is a bit of exaggeration in this statement, but there is no doubt that we need in the United States a nation wide emphasis upon this Bill of Duties idea.

We have over advertised our rights and sadly neglected our duties. For instance, note the millions of voters who fail to vote either at the primaries or at the regular elections. What can be done to make the careless citizen either use his suffrage or face the danger of forfeiture?

But it must not be forgotten that the fathers who wrote the Bill of Rights also included in their vision a

44

Bill of Duties. Accordingly the Constitution gives Congress the right to impose federal taxes, and, in times of emergency, to place drafts upon the person and property of citizens.

Yet, as Mr. Wallace declared, there ought to be in this country a greatly enlarged emphasis upon the idea that American citizenship is a sacred stewardship. With a great price our liberties were bought, so that all of us need to revalue this trust. Especially is this true of both labor and capital.

At this time of national emergency, when the shadow of totalitarianism is lengthening across the world, certainly one of the problems facing all serious minded Americans is how can we maintain the proper equilibrium between the rights and duties of citizens.

In the light of our priceless heritage, a first step would be for each American—worthy of the name—to sit down and formulate his own Bill of Duties!

—RALPH SPAULDING CUSHMAN,
Methodist Bishop,
St. Paul, Minnesota

Renew The Covenant

THE HIGH LIGHT in the life of our young Republic was the belated incorporation of the Bill of Rights into the American Constitution. It is good to know that all Americans are being given the opportunity on December 15th of this year to renew their covenant with the fathers whose wisdom made that document both the pillar of cloud by day and the pillar of fire by night for the guidance of the new conception of government and the American way of life in the Western Hemisphere. Naturally, as a citizen of North Carolina I have a peculiar interest in celebrating the incorporation of freedom of religion, freedom of assembly, freedom of speech and freedom of the press as an integral part in the chart of the American Ship of State. In my judgment the renunciation for a time by North Carolina of enjoying the blessings of the Government to which its people had contributed so generously in blood and treasure, until the Bill of Rights had been incorporated into the greatest instrument ever struck off by the hand of free men, constituted a devotion to principle not surpassed in American annals.

Ten States had ratified the Federal Constitution when the North Carolina Convention met at Hillsboro, July 21, 1788—enough of the States to organize and set the new Government in operation under Washington. After long debate the opponents of ratification declared their firm purpose to incorporate the Bill of Rights into the Constitution before they would enter the union. By a vote of 184 to 84 the Convention virtually said, "Anxious as we are to take our seat in the structure of the new republic of our dreams, the liberties set forth in the Bill of Rights are so essential to the realization of that dream that we demand their incorporation before we ratify."

Those early patriots feared that Federalists might not incorporate the freedoms so dear to their hearts if every colony entered the union before the Bill of Rights was a part of the instrument. They sacrificed their long-cherished desire to take part in the organization of the new government and their laudable ambition to be represented in official position. But above and beyond all other considerations their hearts' desire was for religious freedom and the other freedoms that could be safeguarded only by the adoption of the Bill of Rights. Some of them had felt the stings of religious persecution, and they highly resolved that old world intolerance should be outlawed in the very beginning by the young Republic. No sacrifice was too great— even the renunciation of public office with the honors and emoluments thereunto appertaining.

As soon as this chart of liberty was made an integral part of the Constitution, the North Carolina Convention hastened to ratify and to take its seat with its neighbors in the new Government. Naturally the important offices had been filled and North Carolina's voice in high official station was lost for a time. But by self-sacrifice it had insured the freedom dearer than all else for itself and other commonwealths.

Because of this record, North Carolina will be first in celebrating and in rejoicing in its early devotion to the essential liberties of a democracy and will join with all other Americans in an organized warfare against any lessening of devotion to the principles in the Bill of Rights and any intolerance or denial of its blessings to any people.

—Josephus Daniels,
United States Ambassador to Mexico

The Measure Of Americanism

THE BILL OF RIGHTS, what is it? Is it history, is it rhetoric, is it merely an ancient document entitled to respect because of age; or is it a living force in American life? Did American liberty begin with the adoption of the Bill of Rights, or is it a shield erected to protect the liberty Americans had won? What is the theory of government that makes the Bill of Rights necessary? To whom are its commandments addressed? Put these questions to any reasonably intelligent man and his answers will give you a true measure of his understanding of Americanism.

Undoubtedly the Bill of Rights is history, ancient history, for it draws on long centuries of experience of men and their rulers. Unquestionably it is rhetoric, stirring rhetoric, because of the great ideas its sentences expound. The whole of the American theory of government—human equality, popular sovereignty, personal liberty—can be found in the Preamble of the Declaration of Independence and in the Bill of Rights.

So it is that when the founders of America framed their government they did not go hat in hand to some superior sovereign begging for an expansion of their rights and liberties, for these they and their fathers had already won. They did not need a Bill of Rights either to create their rights or to protect one citizen against another. They adopted it solely to protect themselves against any abuse by the government they had established. Read the Bill of Rights as contained in the first ten amendments to the Constitution and mark how every paragraph is a prohibition, a command that this or that shall *not* be done. Congress "shall make no law" prohibiting the free exercise of religion, or abridging freedom of speech or of the press. The right to bear arms "shall not be" infringed. The right of the people to be secure against unreasonable searches and seizures "shall not be" violated. And so on, and so on.

So it is behind the shield of these and like commandments in the constitutions of the several States that the American people have enjoyed for a century and a half free worship, a free press, free assembly, freedom from search, freedom from self-incrimination, freedom from the confiscation of property, from arbitrary arrest and imprisonment and all the other rights of free and independent men. They have enjoyed these things because the Bill of Rights denies the power of any government—the one set up in 1789 or any other—or of any majority, no matter how large, to invade the native rights of a single citizen.

There was a day when the absence of such rights in other countries could fill an American with incredulous pity. Yet today, over vast reaches of the earth, governments exist that have robbed their citizens by force or fraud of every one of the essential rights American citizens still enjoy. Usage blunts surprise, yet how can we regard without amazement and horror the depths to which the subjects of the totalitarian powers have fallen?

The lesson is plain for all to read. No men enjoy freedom who do not deserve it. No men deserve freedom who are unwilling to defend it. Americans can be free so long as they compel the governments they themselves have erected to govern strictly within the limits set by the Bill of Rights. They can be free so long, and no longer, as they call to account every governmental agent and officer who trespasses on these rights to the smallest extent. They can be free only if they are ready to repel, by force of arms if need be, every assault upon their liberty, no matter whence it comes.

—John W. Davis

Vital Forces Of Humanity

IT IS PARTICULARLY significant that the 150th anniversary of the adoption of the Bill of Rights should come at a time when the freedom of nations and men is again in the world crucible. During recent years the forces of political atavism have destroyed the rights of the individual in nation after nation abroad. Here in our own country, threats have been made against our traditional theories of equality and the dignity of the individual. It is fitting, therefore, that in observing the 150th anniversary of the Bill of Rights, we consider again its meaning and dedicate ourselves anew to the achievement of its enduring purpose.

It was a sign of the health of the young Republic that, in spite of the great ideals enunciated in the Declaration of Independence and the original Constitution, the Bill of Rights was adopted further to clarify the rights of the individual and the States. This was evidence that the young Republic was a moving force for freedom. So long as a government remains responsive to its people and pursues a course designed to promote the healthy growth of individual character, that government is a bulwark of civilization against the inroads of totalitarianism. More than that, it is an aggressive force for freedom everywhere.

Freedom of religion, speech and the press, the right of assembly and all the other civil rights guaranteed in the first ten amendments to the Constitution are vital forces of humanity. A government based on such a philosophy has right on its side. It must prevail against the false philosophies of irreligion, nationalism, class creeds and an individual life that amounts to slavery.

Only on a foundation which recognizes the freedom and well-being of the individual can a lasting and just peace settle upon this troubled world. By re-affirming the principles embodied in the Bill of Rights, we here in America can give new hope to the oppressed peoples abroad and help establish a better world.

—THOMAS E. DEWEY,
*District Attorney of
the County of New York*

To Check Intolerance

I DO NOT BELIEVE there can be any equivocation as to the rights of the American people to think, to speak, and to act as free agents.

If at any time it is the purpose of certain groups or individuals to destroy the Constitution or any of its Amendments, it would seem to me that we as a people should combat them in the open air of public knowledge rather than in the dank and fetid atmosphere of underground activity.

I would be in favor of legislation which would make it obligatory for any individual or group indulging in any kind of propaganda to register with the Government a complete roster of its personnel and a full statement of the source of its finances. Certainly no organization that is not subversive should object to such publicity.

But to begin denying the guarantees of the Bill of Rights to anyone, whatever his intentions, is to open the flood gates of possible persecution. It is so easy for any element of the people to accuse of subversive activity any other element with whom they do not agree, and were it not for the legal guarantees of the

Bill of Rights, there would exist no instrument to check intolerance.

I am fully aware of the danger to our national unity and security which is presented by those who use the democratic guarantees of freedom and the democratic processes to achieve anti-democratic ends. However, there are specific municipal, State and Federal laws relating to actual overt acts of treason, sabotage, etc., under which prosecution can be instituted. I believe that in the combating of subversive activities we must take full advantage of such laws as well as full advantage of the spotlight of publicity which can be thrown on subversive elements. We can also make an honest effort to rid our nation of those social and economic ills which are still to be found in it and which all subversive elements use to create disaffection and dissension.

The Bill of Rights is the lifeblood of our freedom. Let us not tamper with it.

—MELVYN DOUGLAS

The Protecting Mantle

THE FEDERAL CONSTITUTION which was adopted in Philadelphia in 1787 has been described as the most important document emanating at one time from the brain of man. This Constitution sets up the government of the United States of America and furnishes the foundation and framework of what is now the greatest nation on earth.

The first ten Amendments to the Constitution, which have been so expressedly declared the Bill of Rights, are the protecting mantle, under the Constitution, for the people of the country. It was the first expression put into written form by any nation for the protection of the individual rights of its citizens.

It is a remarkable thing, however, that while the Constitution sets up the organized government and these Amendments protect the citizen under that government, yet there is no expression, either in the Constitution or elsewhere, of the citizen's duty to that government. The obligation of the citizen to his government is equal to that of the government to the citizen. He must be the individual guarantor to the nation of similar rights to all citizens of that nation so that the nation's guarantee to him will be fulfilled.

While no one born in the United States is obliged to take an oath of allegiance to the government under the Constitution and the Amendments, yet everyone born elsewhere, seeking citizenship, takes that oath. This places a higher degree of responsibility on the American-born citizen because it is his duty to show, by example to all others, his devotion and allegiance to his government under its Constitution. It is this spirit of responsibility which carries with it tolerance and understanding and makes the real value of American citizenship.

In upholding our Constitution, we must bear and forbear with each other. The more fortunately placed of our citizens must show that consideration to the least of them in order that the guarantee to all shall be equal. With that spirit of brotherhood and common interest and tolerance, our actions toward each other will enhance our citizenship and strengthen our united nation.

—MICHAEL FRANCIS DOYLE

Rights—Not Privileges

TO ME, OUR BILL OF RIGHTS is the formal recognition of civilized man's struggle for the dignity of his soul, his conscience and his person.

When first the Bill came into being it was a re-affirmation of man's faith in the way of life he had been taught was his, as a component part of a society whose government was responsible to him and his fellows alone. Today it is a constant and indestructible reminder that we, the free citizens of a free nation, possess equal opportunity to make of ourselves what we will, within the limits of laws which representatives of our own choosing legislate in our behalf. Furthermore, it is the hope of the hapless, the shield of the unfortunate, the least of whom can claim certain indisputable freedoms.

It is, truly, a Bill of *Rights* and *not* a bill of *privileges*. It is that distinction which gives to the individual his strength and integrity. It is his assurance of his right to aspire. It is the sanctuary to which he can retire, safe against any unwarranted trespassing upon his conception of dignity and decency and political security. It is a proclamation of man's humanity to man.

—DOUGLAS FAIRBANKS, JR.

The Paths Must Be Kept Open

THE THIRTEEN COLONIES justified their claim to a place among the nations of the world by insisting on "the pursuit of happiness" as "an inalienable right." Two thousand years before Jefferson expressed the underlying faith of our American society, Pericles, who was not a stranger to Jefferson's spirit, revealed "the secret of happiness to be freedom." To "secure the Blessings of Liberty to ourselves and our Posterity" the thirteen States formed the Union. The Constitution is thus an instrument of government under which the pursuit of happiness through freedom may be realized. The Bill of Rights, as an organic part of our scheme of government, was not intended as a blueprint of Utopia. Written into the Constitution to guard against the recurrence of well-defined historic grievances, the Bill of Rights was the product not of rhetoric but of experience. The early American statesmen were alive to abuses of arbitrary power which have their seeds in the nature of man and may thrive under any form of government. And so they summarized their experience and made explicit the conditions of freedom —a rational and disinterested procedure when men are accused of crime, prohibition of "unreasonable searches and seizures," freedom of thought and of conscience, and the amplest opportunity for expressing both.

It misconceives however the inner significance of the Bill of Rights to think of it as constituting merely technical provisions of a legal code. An independent, learned, courageous and imaginative judiciary is indispensable to a free society, and especially to a federated democracy. But one does not minimize the role of courts in acknowledging that, for the ultimate protection of the liberties of the people, it is not sufficient to rely on the specialized and very limited function of the judiciary. Litigation is, as it were, the pathological aspect of society. Health comes from the thoughts and feelings permeating its atmosphere and guiding its everyday actions. The real import of the Bill of Rights is the conception of man's dignity and destiny which underlies it, and which can effectively be vindicated only if it controls public feeling and inspires all measures of government.

Lincoln magnificently illustrates that Nature herself is democratic. The arrangements of society should not thwart her purposes. Tolerances for dissident views is not an exercise in benignity but a form of practical wisdom. Truth is an eternal chase. The history of man's endeavor to achieve truth shows the displacement of yesterday's dogma by today's skepticism. And today's folly may prove itself tomorrow's wisdom. The paths to the City of God must be kept open.

The spirit of man and the means for achieving its glories can never be captured and confined by words and formulas. But the framers of the Bill of Rights put into enduring language the conditions essential for the "Blessings of Liberty" to themselves and their posterity. By celebrating their wisdom in this formulation we invigorate our own strength to maintain that liberty. The Founders of the Republic knew, as did Pericles, that if the secret of happiness was freedom "the secret of freedom was a brave heart." Let us be worthy of their example.

—FELIX FRANKFURTER,
Associate Justice,
United States Supreme Court

No Greater Treasure

RECIPIENTS OF GREAT GIFTS too often regard them carelessly or indifferently. It is characteristic of a people that too often they fail to look unto the rock whence they are hewn. A world catastrophe tends to "stab them broad awake." Such a catastrophe faces the free peoples of America today. Privileges and blessings long enjoyed have been threatened and a startled nation is called upon to reappraise its virtues and its vices. Few have heeded or regarded with reverent devotion their great inheritance in the Constitution and particularly in the Bill of Rights. The rights have been assumed without due regard for the cost and sacrifice which they entail. They are accepted, frequently abused by prodigal and unthinking men and women.

What do these accepted freedoms mean to us? Can they be maintained in perpetuity unless we are ready and prepared to defend them at any cost? Can they be transmitted to our children unimpaired if we permit elements within or threatening influences from without to treat them with contempt or to violate their rich provisions?

Apart from my Christian convictions and indeed as

an expression of these convictions, I regard my citizenship under the Constitution and Bill of Rights as a treasure and as a blessing greater than that enjoyed by any citizen of the world, ancient or modern. Freedom of assembly, freedom of speech, freedom of worship, and what comes to me through freedom of the press, constitute a heritage of incalculable value. They lay upon me responsibilities and obligations that call for all that I possess of moral courage and Christian virtue. They compel me to be considerate of the rights and privileges of others. They prescribe generosity, kindness and tolerance in all human relationships. They admonish me that here in free America every citizen is a sovereign whose privileges cannot be infringed by any act of mine. While they accord me freedom of speech they do not permit me to employ it to the hurt of others. While they permit me to enjoy freedom of worship, they inculcate in me a charitable attitude towards those whose traditions and training cause them to pursue a way different from my own.

It is a Bill of Rights that, without discrimination or favor, guarantees to every citizen, life, liberty and the pursuit of happiness. Any attempted abuse or infringement of these rights, any attempt to put restraints upon their free and consistent exercise should deny to the offending citizen the privileges they confer.

—JAMES E. FREEMAN,
Bishop of Washington
Protestant Episcopal Church

Guaranties Against Tyranny

MEMORIES OF THE "days before Hitler" come to us all, now and then with startling vividness, illuminating whole areas of faith and experience. Such is my memory of the way in which I used to accept the truth of the often quoted phrase: "Eternal vigilance is the price of liberty."

This was, it seemed to me, true as a matter of course. But not especially important for me and my generation. For who was there, in the days before the rise of Fascism and Nazism, to challenge liberty? Especially in this country?

And what was liberty, after all? Except something to be talked about by commencement orators, and Congressmen when their remarks were extended in the record, and politicians who felt themselves slipping and had to wave the flag frantically to protect their own fortunes?

"Liberty" connoted all the things we took for granted in our American life, all the things our fathers had to fight to gain, but which we accepted just as we did the right to live, and breathe free air, and go about our several businesses in peace.

Who ever got excited about those rights and privileges? They were unchallenged, had come to us without effort, and were no more regarded than good health. And the only person who values good health is the man who hasn't got it!

So that's how it was with the Bill of Rights. Fine! "The cornerstone of our liberties!" And how's your golf game? Or let's have another drink.

But today—how vastly is the situation changed. When a large part of the world, which enjoyed a measure of individual freedom much the same as ours, has had all its rights and privileges taken away from it, they become tremendously important to us. They are "more precious than rubies," "and all the things thou canst desire are not to be compared" to them.

Now we realize why our fathers, who refused to submit to the tyranny of irresponsible rulers, or to yield control of their lives and fortunes to a government of others' choosing (or to any government) fought not only for the certainties of the Constitution, but for the guaranties of the Bill of Rights.

There are assured to us the freedoms for the individual without which there can be no freedom for the state, no social good, no promise of progress toward the fuller and better life for all.

And we value them the more now that we see them not only challenged and assailed in other parts of the world, but threatened by a tendency on the part of our own government to follow a course which runs counter to the way of life which has made our country what it is.

"Eternal vigilance is the price of liberty!"

—FRANK E. GANNETT

Truths For Our Time

WHEN WE ESPOUSE Democracy as the best form of government and the Bill of Rights as the surest guarantee of our liberties, it is not an arbitrary insistence upon a set of values merely because they were chosen by our fathers a century and a half ago. Americans least of all are tradition-bound. Readily, nay eagerly, we change styles of dress, housing, locomotion and communication; surely we should not continue a form of government merely because our fathers adopted it.

If we espouse the Bill of Rights today, it is because we today, viewing the world of our time, and observing the other kinds of governments which are being tried, have come to our own conclusions that ours is the best for the reason that it offers the most likely means for the attainment of the most worthwhile boons for the largest number of the people.

It must be recognized, however, that the difference between empty phrases and precious principles is to be measured by the price men are willing to pay. To the generation which fashioned the Constitution and the Bill of Rights, these meant much because they cost them much in comfort, blood, life itself. For our generation these principles will take on a vitality of meaning in proportion to the danger by which they are perilled from within and from without, and the price we may have to pay for their preservation.

Much is being said about the risk of losing our freedom in the process of defending it. The converse of the proposition, however, needs also to be recognized, namely, that in the face of Nazi ambitions of world hegemony there is the danger of losing our present form of government, if not our sovereignty—and with it our freedom altogether, if we arbitrarily refuse to yield a fraction of our prerogatives in order to safeguard the general area of our liberties.

What is to be the guiding formula? Obviously, as much freedom as is consistent with the main task. Who is to define the amount and determine the consistency? There can be no arbitrary definition. Every proposal to curtail any of the prerogatives of a free Democracy must be vigilantly scrutinized. We must be realistic enough, however, to distinguish between freedom as a whole and freedom in particular details. There is a hierarchy of values. For the sake of safeguarding the topmost values, those in the lower scale may have to be temporarily yielded. Otherwise, by arbitrary, undiscriminating rigidity, we are in danger of losing the power to defend our liberties as a whole. To urge such a policy would be a counsel of unwitting naiveté or malicious treachery.

For us Americans the democratic way of life is not a device made to order for the purpose of expansion, conquest and war. It is our ennobling heritage which has been tested in a century and a half of national policy, through war and peace, and has not been found wanting.

The history of the United States is the most exciting of all national annals. Ours was a New World in more than one sense. It was a newly discovered continent. It was colonized by men and women who by their coming to the new shores broke with their own past and with many of the traditions of the old society. They and their offspring were psychologically as well as physically free to re-evaluate the social and political conventions of the Old World. They kept what they deemed worthwhile and rejected what they considered obsolete.

This republic of ours was founded with a purpose and a mission, consisting both of protest and affirmation. These were not an afterthought or a post facto rationalization, but an initial propelling motivation.

In the world of stress and challenge in which we live, when the ideas and ideals of Democracy are ridiculed and repudiated in foreign lands and spurned by some who dwell within our own shores, they derive new cogency from the menace of the anti-democratic forces. They are not dead letters but living flaming truths for our time.

We need to recapture the spiritual excitement, the dynamics of idealism, which moved the founders of this nation. Our shining armor has tarnished with the passage of a century and a half, but only the surface has become dulled. With little effort it can be made bright again. We need only to be reminded. The metal is sound, and uncorroded.

We are being told that the new order which threatens to dominate Europe today is a "revolution." No one can predict how far it will go or how long it will endure. Sooner or later it must collapse, because it shackles the mind and chains the spirit of man. Against that kind of "revolution" we Americans set our way of life conceived in a revolution which was marked by the unshackling of fetters which had chained the human spirit.

As soon as we become sufficiently aware of what we have at stake in the present world crisis we shall realize that no sacrifice is too high a price to pay.

—ISRAEL GOLDSTEIN,
Chairman Jewish Section, Inter-faith Committee for Aid to the Democracies

The Rights Of Labor

IN 1935 WITH PASSAGE by Congress of the National Labor Relations Act new meaning was given to the freedom of the individual guaranteed under the Constitution of the United States. The right of workers to join trade unions of their own choosing without fear of discharge or other discrimination by employers has been safeguarded and made a reality by the National Labor Relations Act. Labor has thus been enabled for virtually the first time to deal with employers on terms of equality. With the destruction of democracy in so many European countries, it is of prime importance that Americans retain labor's "Bill of Rights"; that the right to organize for collective bargaining be preserved and strengthened; that the right to strike which distinguishes free labor from captive labor remains unimpaired. We can not have freedom of thought and action otherwise. A strong labor movement is better able to meet its responsibilities in our democracy than is a cowed and weakened body of workers.

—ELINORE M. HERRICK,
Regional Director,
National Labor Relations Board

A Time To Remember

THE UNITED STATES BILL OF RIGHTS is the supreme charter in our time of human liberty. It is the pledge and guarantee in this country—and ultimately, we may pray, in the world at large—of man's inherent right to think his own thoughts, to speak his own ideas, to publish his own opinions, to worship his own God, and to assemble with his fellows to promote his own causes.

It is easy to proclaim these rights, and easy and pleasant to practise them ourselves. The difficulty comes in permitting others to practise them—those, for example, whom we do not like, or whom we deem dangerous to the best interests and perhaps the very safety of the community. Yet it is in the exercise of these rights by the humblest and most hated among us that this charter of human liberty is alone truly vindicated.

It is to be noted that the Bill of Rights is not cumbered by any restrictions, or reservations, or exceptions. It does not say that the rights specified shall be suspended in the case of Negroes, or Jews, or Communists, or Jehovah's Witnesses, or aliens, or other groups whom some men dislike or fear. It does not provide that the rights specified shall be abrogated in times deemed perilous to established interests and institutions. It does not even reserve the rights specified to periods of peace. It states flatly that the rights specified in the Bill shall not be abridged. This means, according to the Supreme Court of the United States, speaking in the Milligan Case after the Civil War:

"The Constitution of the United States is a law for rulers and people, equally in war and in peace, and covers with the shield of its protection all classes of men, at all times, and under all circumstances. No doctrine involving more pernicious consequences was ever invented by wit of man than that any of its provisions can be suspended during any of the great exigencies of government."

This is a good time in which to remember these things.

—JOHN HAYNES HOLMES,
Chairman, Board of Directors,
American Civil Liberties Union

A Tremendous Undertaking

I SOMETIMES THINK that I would have given all the wealth of this great hemisphere if I could have been one of that little band that went out to the field of Runnymede in 1215 and extracted from King John that wonderful collection of human liberties, known as Magna Charta. After liberty had been banished from the world for a thousand years, I repeat, if I could have had the wonderful privilege of being one of that band that thus took the first step back toward human freedom—the first step in that 500-year struggle for Anglo-Saxon liberty—I would have parted with all the wealth of this Western Hemisphere. And I want to see some of that same spirit that finally culminated in our own country in the Revolution and the structure of our free government revived. . . .

We have carried the experiment of self-government further than it has ever been carried in the history of the human race, and yet it remains an experiment. If in this undertaking we should fail, if our civilization should be unable to cope with that age-old problem of self-government, I doubt if it will ever be undertaken again in the future.

So we have the tremendous undertaking today of rebuilding more securely, along political and economic lines, our relationships with the other nations. I think we ought to build upon the solid and broad foundations of justice, equality, and friendship. I think, too, that the more we visualize those broader relationships, both political and economic, that should be restored, keeping at all times within the limitations of our traditions and our Constitution, the greater service we will render to ourselves and to other peoples.

—CORDELL HULL,
United States Secretary of State

Rights Must Be Defended

WHEN, IN 1787, Jefferson, who was American Minister in Paris, received a copy of the draft of the Constitution, he was startled to see that it contained no Bill of Rights. To Jefferson, as well as to many another American democrat, that made no sense. A Constitution without a Bill of Rights was like a gun without ammunition. A Constitution that did not specifically guarantee the basic rights of the individual was not worth the paper it was written on. "A bill of rights," Jefferson said grimly, "is what the people are entitled to against every government on earth." And enlightened opinion throughout America agreed with him.

Today many Americans are inclined to forget that the Bill of Rights that was finally and permanently grafted upon the Constitution entailed a long struggle of about two years. We have preserved those rights over a period of a century and a half because our forefathers have always been willing to fight for them. Rights, especially such precious ones as those that protect our conscience, our opinion, and our physical freedom, are never automatic like a reflex, or God-given like rain. Rights have to be carefully cherished, jealously guarded, and staunchly defended. Rights, no matter how frequently they may be repeated in the statute books, can die of neglect. They can expire as the result of indifference or cowardice. A dramatic illustration of this is the case of the German Republic where the people were either unwilling or unable to defend their freedom. They are now paying for their neglect by untold misery. France furnishes, I think, another example of indifference and neglect. Too many Frenchmen, alas, although sincere democrats at heart, came to believe that their rights and their freedom would defend themselves; in a crisis they were not ready to lay down their lives for their cherished heritage. Now France is crushed and enslaved.

There is a powerful lesson in this for us Americans. We have fought to obtain our liberties. We have fought to preserve our liberties. We will fight to keep them. We Americans know that the price of freedom is still eternal vigilance. We also know that without liberty—without a Bill of Rights—life is not worth the trouble. We Americans love life, and we will see to it that it is not lived on our knees but on our feet.

—HAROLD L. ICKES,
United States Secretary of the Interior

The Condition Of Democracy

NOT MANY YEARS AGO it was easy to find advanced political thinkers who questioned the desirability of any bill of rights. Did not the original English Bill of Rights root in the conception that the individual needed a sphere of his own, immune to the attacks of the monarch, regarded as a will possibly above, possibly below that of the generality, but in any event separate from it? With the triumph of the democracy, what need had the individual for protection against the government, representing himself?

There is no advanced thinker who talks this way nowadays. We have seen in Russia, Italy, and Germany what life is like for the individual who has no Bill of Rights to defend him. The will of the majority offers no protection to the individual belonging to the minorities. We have been compelled to recognize that the conventional conception of the minority, as a group differing in no essentials from the majority and which may at any time become the majority, is unrealistic. The problem of today is one of the rights of members of persistent minorities—religious minorities like the Catholics, Jews, Quakers, Mormons, Free

Thinkers; racial and national minorities such as abound on the borders of every European state and are also to be found abundantly in America; political and economic minorities, such as the Reds, the liberals, and the reactionaries, organized labor and the bourgeoisie.

Without a bill of rights no minority is secure against persecution. No individual can be sure that his particular group will not find itself in the position of a proscribed minority. Our lives, our liberties, our happiness are at the mercy of the squalls and flurries of opinion, unless we are adequately protected by a bill of rights and a truly independent judiciary.

A bill of rights is in one sense a curb upon democracy. But in another sense it is the condition of the permanence of democratic institutions. No democracy can long exist if one group after another may be thrust into the position of a minority to be extirpated. Greek democracy perished for want of a bill of rights insuring a modicum of security for the individual. Russia and Germany are modern examples of polities inadequately equipped with a bill of rights, hence devastated by recurring purges and the enforced order of dictatorship.

—ALVIN JOHNSON,
Director,
The New School of Social Research

For All Men

INTOLERANCE BROUGHT about the holocaust which now threatens the world.

The people of the United States have pledged their efforts to see that this threat is removed. They believe in the Bill of Rights not only for themselves but for all of those who live on this earth.

They look forward with hope and conviction to the day when intolerance and the forces which create it will have been completely eradicated.

—JESSE JONES,
United States Secretary of Commerce

Beacons To The World

THE ANNIVERSARY of the adoption of the Bill of Rights as a part of the Constitution recalls to mind how the Bill got only late into the Constitution as well as the significance it now has there for life and liberty.

Those who made the Constitution had seen during the period from 1776 to 1787 such weakness of national government that in their desire for "a more perfect union" they over-stressed the institutional aspect in the structure they created, with consequent threat to personality and freedom, on the one hand, and neglect of the proper methods of effecting intelligent social change, on the other. The Bill of Rights was thus put into the Constitution four years later in order to correct this over-emphasis on the institutional and safeguard the essential interests otherwise threatened.

The Bill of Rights means then at bottom the reassertion of essential democracy along two complementary lines. The first is the safeguarding of human personality, at once source and end of human rights, as over against the natural dangers inherent in the ever necessary habit-institutionalizing aspect and tendency of life. The second is the safeguarding of free discussion and inquiry as the indispensable means for maintaining the continual adequacy of our cultural content and institutional machinery.

Institutions as the patterns of effectual human interaction are essential to the development and expression of human life and personality. Habits fix these helpful patterns in men for more effective intercourse. Institutions and habits come thus initially into being in answer to prevailing conditions. They may, therefore, as conditions change, go out of date and become harmful instead of helpful. Continual revision of institutions is accordingly necessary to keep them abreast of needs and conditions. But habit works to oppose revision and especially so where the out-of-date institution protects vested interests.

It is under such circumstances that the Bill of Rights best serves, namely to protect those who are foremost to sense some unnecessary evil and seek appropriate institutional changes to remedy it. With entrenched habit and privilege supporting the status quo, those who advocate such change may meet not only opposition but even suppression and at times persecution besides, unless and until the Constitution through the courts brings the protecting Right into effective play. So the Bill works in our country, and never perhaps better than now.

But our Bill of Rights reaches in influence beyond the boundaries of our own country. In these evil days, when human rights are cruelly denied over so much of the world, these Rights stand out, with those of Great Britain, as beacons to the world to stir the hopes and guide the thinking of the distressed peoples, to hold up before them the ever continuing possibility of life and liberty based on justice and respect for human personality. When this war shall come to an end and Hitlerism is finally destroyed, the substance of our Bill of Rights must furnish the foundation for a new and better society, a society in which all men are treated as persons on terms of ethical equality, entitled to share effectively in making the policies that rule them, protected in their rights as free men to think and speak and vote each as his own mind and conscience shall direct him. Thus the Bill can and must work elsewhere, and never perhaps more urgently so than now.

—WILLIAM HEARD KILPATRICK,
Professor Emeritus, Teachers College,
Columbia University

A Call To Duty

EQUALITY BEFORE THE LAW and civil and religious liberty are inalienable rights guaranteed by our Constitution to all. But freedom by law is freedom in practice only where the law is sustained by public opinion and the will to sacrifice.

Men talk glibly of democracy as if it were something that could be bought in the market place—something to provide soft living and freedom from toil and danger. That is not the fabric of which true democracy is made. That is not the democracy for which men have nobly died. True democracy is an expression of faith—a vital and dynamic force—a call to duty from which we do not draw back. Democracy, like religion, must be supported by a militant faith in the things that are right and good and just—a faith that calls for courage and devotion and sacrifice.

That is what American democracy means to most of us. As someone has truly said, "Our freedoms have only been loaned to us." They remain our permanent possession only so long as we show ourselves worthy of them. We must match privileges with corresponding loyalties. We must impose upon ourselves as a free people voluntary self-discipline, more compelling and more effective than ruthless decree of dictators.

The United States was founded to assert human rights. Our Flag means an heroic enterprise of man's spirit of brotherhood. Our Declaration of Independence and the Bill of Rights are compelling expressions of the religious concept of justice and equality.

Men proclaim that America is the greatest and noblest country of the world. We know that it is. But America will remain great only if its spirit remains great. America will remain noble only if its people have clean hearts and an unshakeable will to stand for the right and the just, regardless of sacrifice or risk. Instead of saying, "I am an American and therefore I have *rights*," each one of us should be proud to say, "Because I am an American, I have a *solemn duty* to maintain the ideals of morality and justice for which America has ever stood and which have been the basis of our greatness."

—HERBERT H. LEHMAN,
Governor of New York

A Pressing Responsibility

IT IS A STRANGE LAW of life that one never appreciates the meaning of physical health until one has lost it in whole or in part. So with social and political organisms. Only when freedom has been infringed or lost do most people begin to appreciate its value.

The priceless boon which we enjoy under the Bill of Rights is something far too many of us take for granted. Were we more alert to observe world trends, we would wake with a start to see that almost everywhere such rights have ceased to be. They are founded upon the Judaeo-Christian concept of man as the creature of God endowed by him with certain inalienable rights. It is a significant fact that where that concept is abandoned the next step seems to be an abandonment of the view of human society upon which the basic freedoms depend. Our task is to preserve both and to do it by a realistic method calculated to meet the spiritual and physical risks of the present crisis.

What are those risks? The first and most dangerous grows out of the attitude of those Americans who assume that these freedoms are not in need of defense, that they are self-perpetuating or natural in some automatic sense.

A further risk is that failing to see their essential spiritual basis we shall consider them a mere matter of techniques in jurisprudence.

A third risk is that we shall succumb to extraordinary pressures of this world crisis against human freedom and destroy it in a mistaken effort to save it.

A fourth risk—balanced over against the third—is that we should refuse such temporary limitation of freedom by free consent as is necessary for its total defense.

To confront these and other dangers is a pressing responsibility of free government guided by the common sense of a free people aware of the things which today menace their heritage.

—HENRY SMITH LEIPER,
Foreign Secretary,
The Federal Council of the
Churches of Christ in America

Freedom—A Holy Word

MY FATHER, A DANISH peasant, chose this country for his permanent home. Among the qualities of American life which he cherished most, freedom stood at the top. He thought of the Bill of Rights as a kind of holy word. One thing I remember well of his reverence: he was accustomed to say that in a country with a Bill of Rights, no man would ever be required to become a conspirator; each man could stand in dignity and say his word, whether it be the word of praise or the word of discontent which seeks improvement; never would he need to seek a subterranean channel, for the state itself had guaranteed his basic rights. I can still remember the glow upon his countenance as he spoke to newly-arrived immigrants concerning this charter for free men.

So I feel also.

It has been one of my tasks in recent years to strive for the defense of American citizens whose civil rights have been somehow, usually through error or perversity, impaired. I consider this to be one of the most important functions I can perform as a citizen. So long as the arch of freedom remains as the support for these wide-flung federated states we shall enjoy the benefits of Democracy. And, if ever that arch begins to crumble, we shall need to prepare ourselves for tyranny.

—EDUARD C. LINDEMAN,
Professor of Social Philosophy,
New York School of Social Work,
Columbia University

A Shining Charter

THE BILL OF RIGHTS, as I view it, is like the Constitution of the United States of which it is essentially a part, a shining charter for democracy. It is, however, obviously a goal to be aimed at and by no means as yet an accomplished mode of procedure. The Bill of Rights is violated in tens of thousands of cases daily in this Democracy. Men and women are fined and jailed without due process of the law because they are poor or because they are Jews or Mexicans or Negroes. Nearly every state and particularly the southern tier violate—by poll tax or literacy tests or plain shut-outs—the individual right of American citizens to vote in every election.

At the very time when this arsenal of Democracy is clamoring for skilled workmen, citizens of colored skin, yellow, brown, or black, are barred from desperately needed service. The American Navy and Marine forces, putting on a powerful drive to recruit officers and men to man the many ships in building, refuse citizens of color any right to serve except as domestics.

In a land devoted to education and to the inalienable right of every citizen to learn all that he can within his capacity, schools for minorities have shorter terms, worse paid teachers, more dilapidated plants and less equipment.

What this all tots up to may be summed up in the comment of an Englishman, a wise man who has studied at first-hand both Europe and America for a half century. He says, "The hell that has broken loose in the world now can be traced directly to mal-treatment and to mis-treatment of minorities. Hitler cannot win because he is taking the same tack. I warn you in the United States that, unless you follow your Bill of Rights more quickly and more clearly and posi-tively than you have yet done, you will in fifty years brew the greatest civil war the world has ever seen."

With all our three billion dollar expenditure for schools and a several billion dollar expenditure for churches, the thinking of American boys and girls, men and women, still lags far behind both their scien-tific and religious training. Religion declares the brotherhood of man and the essential worth and dig-nity of every individual. And yet even the trained preachers of the church, and to a greater extent their congregations, violate often the right of freedom of worship and the concept of brotherhood and per-sonal worth. Ask most Protestants how they feel about their brothers, the Catholics and the Jews, the Christian Scientists, and the Buddhists, and you get the answer.

Scientists, learned specialists in anatomy, physiology, anthropology, psychology, and education have proved that there are no fundamental group differences in American citizens and that, therefore, every child, every man or woman viewed scientifically differs from other children or men and women only in his fundamental abilities, interests, attitudes, and skills, never on the basis of his race, color, or sex. And yet with all this scientific training the product of our schools and colleges persist in and spread the notion that American, Mexican, Chinese, Filipino, Negro groups are "different."

Just as the Magna Charta of England was a bill of rights to protect the nobles from the iron control of monarchs and as the Magna Charta has had to be reinterpreted over and over again to reach down to the English commoner, so our Bill of Rights in the United States must be reinterpreted and continuously enlarged to protect all minorities whatsoever, and to give them justice.

I was much struck by Vice President Wallace's point of view and agree with him that a Bill of Duties must be widely absorbed by the American public and that for every right there is a duty. I conclude that the first of these duties is that of every American citizen who enjoys a right to see to it that every other citizen enjoys the same right.

—MALCOLM S. MACLEAN,
President, Hampton Institute

Cornerstone Of Our National Greatness

THE IDEALS OF FREEDOM and respect for the individual in the life of the Nation have never been expressed more eloquently or more simply than by George Washington. In a letter written shortly after his first inauguration, he said in part, "The citizens of the United States of America have a right to applaud themselves for having given to mankind examples of an enlarged and liberal policy, a policy worthy of imitation. All possess alike liberty of conscience and immunities of citizenship. It is now no more that toleration is spoken of, as if it was by the indulgence of one class of people, that another enjoyed the exercise of their inherent natural rights. For happily, the Government of the United States which gives to bigotry no sanction, to persecution no assistance, requires only that they who live under its protection should demean themselves as good citizens, in giving it on all occasions their effectual support."

"To bigotry no sanction, to persecution no assistance"! That clarion call for brotherhood is deep-rooted in our history—a source of our national greatness. Three centuries ago we were a haven of refuge from the intolerance of the Old World. The early Pilgrims have been joined by representatives of all the oppressed peoples of the world, and here each group has given the best in its culture and its racial stock as its contribution to the America we glory in today.

Out of their experience, the founders of our Government created the finest instrument for freedom and tolerance in the history of practical government —the Constitution.

The responsibility for forging this new form of government for democratic life in America was entrusted to the most astute and experienced leaders in the nation. Years of unhappy experience under colonial government and the Articles of Confederacy had taught them many valuable lessons. After two years of profound deliberation, that momentous document was at last ready to be submitted to the States for ratification.

At once the voice of the people made clear that organization was not enough. While the Constitution, establishing the new form of government, was accepted, the people whose government it was demanded explicit recognition of the fundamental and inalienable rights of man. Within a year after all the States had accepted the Constitution, the first ten amendments were added to give expression to this popular demand. By this "Bill of Rights," the Spirit of the American people was breathed into the body of the law and our great democratic government stirred to life.

The full implication of the principles of human association, thus guaranteed in the fundamental law of the land, had to be worked out in history. Through more than a century and a half, this Bill of Rights has been a beacon light in our social development. We have faced the pitfalls of racialism, of sectionalism, and of economic division, and today this nation, welded into a unity of life and purpose, is a vital testimony of the unerring wisdom of our democratic faith.

One hundred and sixty-five years is not a long period in the course of history and yet the United States has grown from a loosely federated group of thirteen little colonies on the eastern seaboard to a great nation, ranking foremost in standards of living, in scientific achievement, and in political freedom. Materialists may attribute this entirely to a wealth of natural resources, but that does not explain the greatness of the American nation. The use of these resources has been tempered by the various gifts of personality welded into our common life. But again, those rich human resources are not enough to explain American greatness. Conditions of American life have called upon hidden potentialities in individuals as they have felt the bracing tonic of hope and reward for effort. What is it that has given Americans, irrespective of race, creed, or national origin, this right to hope and this expectation of reward for devotion to the common good? For the answer, we must look to those fundamental principles on which our national life is built, as embodied in our Bill of Rights. This is the framework which has made possible the fullest utilization of our resources, both natural and human. This is the safeguard of our rights and liberties which has released tremendous forces of dynamic energy. This is the cornerstone of our national greatness.

—PAUL V. McNUTT,
Administrator,
Federal Security Agency

The Real Test

IT IS OFTEN SAID that the Bill of Rights is the effective safeguard of democracy against all threats of totalitarian encroachment arising within the body politic; as long as it remains a part of our basic law, we need not fear that our cherished freedoms will be destroyed by the enemies of democracy within our own frontiers. I doubt if this is true. The real test of democracy is not applied by asking questions about the statements embodied in a nation's constitution or the presence or absence of ballot boxes and universal suffrage. If anyone wants to know whether the community, state or nation, in which he resides, is truly democratic, let him ask this question: What actually happens to the member of an unpopular minority when he dares to speak his mind in opposition to the spokesmen of the popular majority?

In other words, the Bill of Rights is merely the verbal crystalization of an idea. It is the idea that must be cherished. Unless its principles are actually practiced in the daily life of the citizen, whether he be judge or alderman, governor or president, policeman or school superintendent, administrator or coordinator, employer or employee, labor organizer or personnel officer, commissioner or devoid of any title whatsoever, the words and phrases lose their power, democracy decays, and freedom dies.

To put into practice the principles embodied in the Bill of Rights is increasingly difficult in America these days, not so much because of the threat of Hitler's mechanized might as because of the inevitable trend in the process of organizing mankind into a world community. The political state is becoming a social-service state in all countries; preparations for war and defense only accelerate the process, they have not initiated it. With extension of governmental control over many individual activities with which the state had not previously been concerned, there is increased necessity for the preservation of those fundamental rights to which the true American holds undying allegiance and at the same time a greater strain upon both his emotions and his intellect as he seeks to maintain that loyalty. But regardless of the difficulties that now beset us, there is no escape from the conclusion: only as the soul-satisfying principles of our Bill of Rights are put into effective operation in all departments of our lives can the age-old paradox of the individual in society be resolved in terms of adequate freedom for each person within the limits imposed by the restraints necessary for coordinating all activity within the organized community.

—KIRTLEY F. MATHER,
*Professor of Geology,
Harvard University*

Heartbeat Of The Republic

TAKE AWAY FROM US the guarantees of freedom of speech, press and assembly; security against unlawful search and seizure; due process of law; trial by jury; and protection against cruel and unusual punishments, and what would you have? You would have tyranny, dictatorship, and human enslavement.

No free Government could survive without these guarantees. Where they have been abrogated, human misery has consistently followed.

We have these guarantees here and they have kept us free.

They are contained in the Bill of Rights.

We must never tamper with them nor forget them because they are the keys to freedom and freedom is more important than life itself.

Can you imagine a country where you would be in mortal terror of speaking freely to the members of your own family? Where listening to certain radio programs would be a high crime? Where men and women are shot or sent to concentration camps without the opportunity to speak in their own defense? Where all newspapers must cravenly agree to a dictated policy of Government? Where your every word and action is under watchful suspicion?

Well, there are countries like that today. But they haven't a Bill of Rights. The Governments of those countries have tried to snuff out of men's minds and hearts the last spark of resistance to despotism. They will never succeed because man has an insatiable urge for freedom. Time and again he has shaken off the bonds of serfdom. Not always has he thereafter chosen the difficult route to lasting liberty but he keeps striving in that direction.

Here, 150 years ago, our forefathers fought for and founded a new Nation. They meant it to be a brave, self-respecting land of opportunity and equality. They did their work well.

Today, the economic and cultural superstructure of freedom built on the firm foundation of the Bill of Rights is testimony to the world that initiative, security, and happiness are derivatives of human liberty.

In this fateful year of 1941, our happy way of life is under challenge by a combination of foreign tyrants who mislead their people and who thirst for world domination. Their warped consciences permit them to despise the god-given rights of their fellowmen.

It is our task to see to it that the forces of Democracy are kept stronger than the forces of Despotism.

Our Bill of Rights means everything to us today. It is more than a symbol. It is the very heartbeat of this great Republic. Since it has unfortunately become necessary to do so, we will keep that heart of America beating soundly by fortifying it with the greatest mechanized military might in all the history of the world.

We are engaged in the task of keeping ourselves free. We will never be given a bigger job. We must do it well.

–JAMES M. MEAD,
United States Senator

The Danger Of Prejudice

WE IN AMERICA make no extravagant claims for Democracy. Democratic government will not work miracles. However, under our Constitution and under its first ten Amendments, the integrity of the American individual is better protected than under any other instrument of government. In fact, for more than a century and a half, our civil rights have found the most perfect guarantee against interference yet devised.

Sometimes, due to prejudice and passion, the provisions of the Constitution and the Bill of Rights can be nullified. Public opinion can often be mobilized to such an extent that individual citizens fail to express themselves through fear. Prejudice is the greatest enemy of our American institutions.

Our whole system of education should be directed toward one end: that of keeping the minds of our people free from prejudice, to develop their capacity for rejecting those doctrines which are injurious to our institutions and accepting only those which will strengthen them. Only through freedom of the press, freedom of speech, freedom of assembly and freedom of worship can that capacity be developed. Once the minds of the majority of the American people become closed, our Bill of Rights will be of no avail.

—NEWBOLD MORRIS,
*President of the Council
of the City of New York*

Worth Fighting For

TO ME THE LIBERTIES guaranteed by our Bill of Rights represent those things which are most worth sacrificing for, fighting for, and, if necessary, dying for. They are ideals which liberty-loving citizens are constantly endeavoring to convert into actualities. They are the spiritual basis of our democracy.

In so-called normal times, when there is relative freedom from controversy and crisis, there is almost universal acceptance of the principles of freedom enunciated in our Bill of Rights. But when dangers threaten, when important decisions have to be made, and when there are differences of opinion on important issues, the faith of men in these democratic principles is tested. Some sincere individual would suspend the Bill of Rights as a means of protecting democracy in time of crisis. They fail to recognize that the dangers they would avert and the abuses they would correct are insignificant as compared with the disillusionment, the loss of morale, and the destruction of national unity that would follow such action.

Democracy has an obligation to protect itself against those who would seek to destroy it, whether they be internal enemies or foreign aggressors. But in its effort to protect itself democracy must not destroy those democratic liberties which it is trying to protect. If we do that we will have lost the battle before it begins. Democratic decisions and democratic actions are slower than are those of totalitarian states, thus giving to the latter an initial advantage. It is this fact that causes many honest and loyal citizens to lose faith in democratic processes in time of crisis. We must accept that handicap with full confidence that a united people true to its faith in the principles that made it great is more important than the temporary advantage of a surprise attack.

When the men and the movements that would destroy democracy have passed from the world scene, as they must inevitably do, the spirit of democracy will still live. Our Bill of Rights is the best expression of that spirit that has ever been fashioned by the minds and hearts of men. So long as we retain our faith in those great freedoms incorporated in our Bill of Rights we will have the morale and the unity of purpose that are essential to the protection of democracy.

—Alonzo F. Myers,
   Chairman,
   Department of Higher Education,
   New York University

Our Most Precious Possession

WHAT DOES THE Bill of Rights mean to me? In this
150th year since its adoption, the Bill of Rights could
not mean more than it has always meant to me; but
the great fundamental rights to civil liberties which
it established as a part of the Constitution of the
United States are now more appreciated by me, and
surely by all other loyal American citizens, than at
any other period in our lives. This because of the present crisis in the world's history, when all civil liberties, even the semblance thereof, are being crushed
and their defenders crucified in other parts of the
world, while we face the threat that the same thing
could happen here. The efficient war machines of dictators of Europe and Asia, whose aggressions have
buried in blood the national and civic rights of the
peoples of other nations, are on the march. These dictators openly declare that their war objectives are to
rule the world by force and establish a slavery to
totalitarianism which proclaims contempt for democracies and for every principle of our most precious
heritage, the American Bill of Rights. Not only by
force of arms, but also by insidious propaganda, de-

ceit, lies, fraud, sabotage, and every device which criminal methods can conceive, do they carry on their purpose to rule the world and destroy human liberties.

The Bill of Rights makes American citizenship the most precious possession of the individual. This realization should inspire American unity in preparing to the utmost our physical and moral strength.

The Bill of Rights means the peoples' freedom from tyranny, their freedom for self-government, and in the exercise of that freedom to establish any form of government and any order of economy which the people, through democratic processes, may determine is best for the economic and social welfare of themselves and their posterity.

—CULBERT L. OLSON,
Governor of California

Our Common Defense

THROUGH A CENTURY and a half of turbulent world history, the United States Constitution has proved itself to be the most effective instrument ever devised for the protection of the individual citizen. Yet never before has its strength been felt as in this present struggle for the preservation of democracy and civilization against the forces of paganism and barbarism.

The strength of America lies in our democratic institutions. Our democracy, itself, is the strongest kind of national defense, because it is something that we are willing to fight for, if necessary. So long as the Bill of Rights is preserved as an integral part of our Constitution, neither Nazism nor Communism nor Fascism—no matter how effectively disguised—can gain a foothold in America.

The right guaranteed by our Constitution of "life, liberty and the pursuit of happiness," has a deep significance. Life in America does not mean mere existence. It means living. Liberty means not only freedom in political matters, it means economic liberty and religious liberty. We, who believe in the pursuit of happiness, know that nowhere in the world is the lot of the people happier than under the American way of living.

It is well for all of us in these times to reflect on the content of the Bill of Rights—the right to worship as we choose, the right to free speech, the right of free assembly, the right of free press, the right of equal protection under our laws without class or racial discrimination. Then to compare our heritage, as Americans, to the lot of millions of conquered or conquering people in Europe or Asia today.

If we are to preserve the Bill of Rights, we must be ever on the watch to fight undemocratic forces. The saboteurs of democracy do not attack it as such. Some of them use the slogan "Divide and Rule." They try to stimulate discord and enmity by attacking some one phase of our democratic system—the foreign born citizen, the alien, some race or religion. One group is encouraged to suspect another—a sly word against one religion here, a mean phrase against one race there. But true Americans know that an attack on any race or religion, on any group or class is an attack on democracy. If the Bill of Rights is to serve one, it must serve all—the Gentile and the Jew, the new immigrant and the stranger within our gates, the worker and the industrialist, the white man and the Negro.

Full appreciation of the Bill of Rights—its importance to each one of us as an individual and its significance today to Americans and to the world—is one of the greatest forces that can be exerted for the common defense of American ideals and the American way of life.

—CHARLES POLETTI,
Lieutenant Governor of New York

The Right Of Sacrifice

THE BILL OF RIGHTS is far more than a collection of guarantees; it is an exhortation to a quality of citizenship. For democracy to persist, there must persist the kind of people who established it.

The men who achieved the independence of the United States recognized freedom as the one quality in a social order that is worth every sacrifice necessary to attain it. For freedom they were eager to dare greatly, to fight against overwhelming odds, to give their fortunes and their lives. Their conception of the destiny they intended for the United States was as venturesome and dangerous as it was idealistic.

The ten paragraphs of the Bill of Rights are a reminder that men went cold and hungry, that their bare feet left blood stains across the snow, that they hugged the holy ideal of liberty to their hearts in spite of all the odds that lay against them, in spite of suffering, deprivation and discouragement.

They did these things, not that we might enjoy freedom without risk or service, but that we might sacrifice for its maintenance as they sacrificed for its establishment. The man who possesses liberty possesses the jewel of greatest price, and all the thievedom of the world will burn to take it from him. There is never any let-up in the conflict between just men, seeking to retain freedom, and thieves, seeking to command the will of others. There must never be any let-up in the readiness of free people to do whatever needs to be done to cherish their independence. Implicit in the American Bill of Rights is a guarantee that transcends all the others: "The right of sacrifice in the cause of freedom is reserved to all the people."

—JAMES P. POPE,
Director,
Tennessee Valley Authority

Chart And Compass

THE PRINCIPLE OF EQUALITY is the heart of the Bill of Rights, and the Bill of Rights is the heart of American democracy. Under the aegis of the Bill of Rights, there is no place for discriminations on account of race, color, religion or national origin. Verily, the Bill of Rights is the chart and compass of American liberty.

But the democratic ideals, heritages, traditions and faiths envisioned and expressed in the Bill of Rights are yet to be even approximately realized and transformed into the American Way, practice, pattern and policy in relation to the Negro people. In very truth, the Negro people who are the most disadvantaged, exploited, oppressed and victimized of all of the minority groups is by that very token the true test of the Bill of Rights and the American democratic system.

However, while the Negro is still in the process of fighting to complete the bourgeois, liberal, democratic, political revolution symbolized in the Civil War, which was expected to achieve for him the full stature of American citizenship outlined in the Bill of Rights, without this great and noble body of principles, his struggle for economic, political and social liberation would be well-nigh impossible.

It is for this reason that the Negro must be concerned with, and join the fight for, the complete destruction of all forms of totalitarianism, and especially the menacing evil and danger of Hitler and Hitlerism, and seek with all his might to maintain and preserve American and world democracy.

> —A. Philip Randolph,
> *International President,*
> *Brotherhood of Sleeping Car Porters*

Permanent As The Republic

THE BILL OF RIGHTS, safeguarding as it does the freedom of the American citizen, is our most precious heritage.

Built into the very framework of the Constitution, its provisions are as permanent as the Republic itself and their scope is as wide as the range of lawful human activities.

For a century and a half in the United States religious freedom has been unchallenged, freedom of speech unlimited, the press has received and disseminated the news of the world, and without let or hindrance the people have assembled for free discussion. The person of every citizen has been safe from irregular legal proceedings and his goods from unlawful seizure.

The American can not remember when he did not enjoy these freedoms and he can not conceive that he might be deprived of them.

It is not only appropriate but vitally important that occasions such as the 150th anniversary of its adoption should bring the Bill of Rights into the forefront of our thinking and that a grateful people should recognize it as a source of their liberty, acclaim the faith in mankind which inspired its authors and solemnly undertake to justify that faith by unswerving loyalty to country and to the cause of Democracy in the world.

—Ruth Bryan Owen Rohde,
*Former United States Minister
to Denmark*

Important As Ever

NEVER BEFORE IN HISTORY has the Bill of Rights meant more than it does today. It is important that everyone be conscious of the rights which are guaranteed to our citizens under that Bill of Rights.

If we are familiar with this document, it will curb our prejudices and we will not discriminate against any one because of race or religion.

If we hope to preserve Democracy in this country, we must realize how important it is to see that the rights of all citizens are guarded carefully.

If we allow certain groups to suffer because they are weaker than others, we will find our whole structure of liberty is undermined. Who is to say which groups may become the minority, or the weaker ones in the course of the years?

Read the Bill of Rights as part of the Sesquicentennial Celebration and insist that it is as important to us today as it ever was.

—ELEANOR ROOSEVELT

Natural Rights

The Declaration of Independence proclaims the existence of natural rights when it asserts that "all men are created equal and are endowed by their Creator with certain inalienable rights." While the Bill of Rights does not explicitly mention natural rights, it is closely related to them in two ways: first, most of the rights which it lays down are not only civil but natural rights; second, the presence of the Bill of Rights in the Constitution shows that the members of the Constitutional Convention believed it to be a group of natural rights. The former proposition will be denied only by those who reject entirely the doctrine of natural rights. The latter proposition will seem evident to any one who considers the difference between a legislative statute and a provision of our organic law.

If our Founding Fathers did not believe that the guarantees contained in the Bill of Rights were also natural rights, they would not have taken the trouble to put them into the Constitution. They would have left them at the disposition of the Congress. To be sure, they knew that the people could amend the

Constitution and consequently would be able to abolish the Bill of Rights, but they were well aware that the amending and eliminating process would face much greater practical difficulties than would the enactment of a congressional statute. In other words, the men who drew up the Bill of Rights went as far as they could toward putting them beyond the power of government to take away.

At this time, if not at all times, the most important and valuable portions of the Bill of Rights are the first and fifth articles. Freedom of religion, freedom of speech, freedom of the press, freedom of assemblage and petition are fundamental, as against the arbitrary action of rulers. They are at the opposite pole from the underlying principles of a totalitarian state.

All the provisions of article five are precious to the individual, but the most beneficent is the due process clause. Not merely no citizen, but, no person "shall be deprived of life, liberty or property without due process of law." In its primary acceptation, this clause guarantees to every accused person a hearing, a fair trial. It protects even the poorest and lowliest against arbitrary action by sheriffs, policemen, governors, and other administrative officers. This is procedural due process. The second, or legislative, meaning of the clause has indeed been perverted by interpretation so as to safeguard economic oppression. That is, it has conferred upon the economically powerful and unscrupulous the liberty to injure the economically weak under the guise of free contract. Minimum wage laws and shorter hour laws have been declared unconstitutional on the ground that they deprive the citizens of due process of law. Happily, recent decisions of the Supreme Court have explicitly reversed that canon of interpretation. For some time to come, at any rate, the due process clause will be used only to protect genuine rights, not to sanction the abuse of rights by the powerful.

—JOHN A. RYAN,
Director, Department of Social Action,
National Catholic Welfare Conference

We The People

ANNIVERSARIES OF MANY famous events in the growth of our country still stir our patriotism, but the issues and the conflicts which led to most of them have disappeared between the covers of dusty history books. Enactment of the Bill of Rights is one of the most important developments in our history, yet one which at the same time is a vital, living issue.

"Bill of Rights" is a phrase synonymous with the freedom which we enjoy today. The English Bill of Rights, drawn up just two hundred and fifty years ago, was the backlog of our fight for independence. The Massachusetts Bill of Rights was the forerunner of federal union. And our national Bill of Rights was the instrument which has given life and lasting endurance to our Constitution.

Today, thanks to those written guarantees, we are a free people. But in these distressing times, there are forces at home and abroad which threaten to undermine our fundamental liberties. Our representative, democratic system is a government of law. There is only one other form of authority and that is a government of force. One signifies justice and liberty; the other, tyranny and oppression. We see what has happened in the totalitarian countries where dictators have begun by crushing freedom of the press and the individual liberties of citizens. We must not permit any such encroachments here.

The question is a living issue because with the best motives to protect us against subversive influences, groups of our citizens are tempted to apply suppression, which elsewhere has led to dictatorships. It is a living issue because a government, in making itself strong enough to deal with national problems, sometimes approaches the dictatorial borderline and, in developing collective action, may find it hard not to stifle individual liberty. It is a living issue because modern industrial relations bring many rights into conflict with each other.

Sometimes checks and balances irk us, but in the long run, they provide the majority of us with a maximum of liberty and happiness. That is what the Bill of Rights guarantees. If we all are fair and tolerant in our views and opinions, are honest with ourselves and with others, then "we the people" need never fear our future.

—LEVERETT SALTONSTALL,
Governor of Massachusetts.

For The Protection Of Minorities

THE CONSTITUTION of the United States, before the adoption of the ten Amendments referred to as the Bill of Rights, consisted mainly of the form of government and made provision for the apportionment of representatives. It dealt with the manner and method of passing bills, as well as the general powers of Congress, the setting up of the three coordinate branches of government, the Executive, the Legislative and the Judicial. It further dealt with the compensation of the President, the form of oath, the conferring of power to appoint Ambassadors and inferior officers, crimes against the federal government, extradition between the several states, the method of admitting new States to the union and dealt with the manner and method of amending the document.

It was not, however, until the first ten Amendments, referred to as the Bill of Rights, were adopted that life, strength and vigor were given to the promises made in the Declaration of Independence. It might well be said that before the adoption of these ten Amendments, the Constitution dealt with government whereas the Amendments dealt with the citizens. They are the guarantee of their freedom of speech, of religion, of the press and the right to petition. They were enacted for the protection of minorities and of individuals. They are the soul of the Constitution and it is fitting and proper that time be set aside for the celebration of the anniversary of their adoption. They made the Constitution as near a perfect document as human ingenuity could devise.

—Alfred E. Smith,
Ex-Governor of New York

Basic Human Rights

WHAT IS THE FREEDOM to which under the Bill of Rights and the laws and traditions of America, the American citizen believes he has the right? 1. The freedom to form and hold his own opinions without coercion. 2. The freedom to express and propagate his own opinions within the bounds of American law and tradition, with no advocacy of change of the laws and traditions except by orderly and peaceful process. 3. Equal laws and equality before the law for every citizen and for every group of citizens. 4. Freedom from all discriminatory legislation, favorable or unfavorable, affecting religious, educational or charitable agencies, whether Protestant, Roman Catholic or Jewish.

These freedoms we desire for ourselves and ought to desire for all men. Whoever, for example, claims freedom for religious minorities in America ought to claim similar freedom for religious minorities in Spain and Russia and Germany. The rights recognized in the Bill of Rights were not created by that Bill. They are basic human rights which all men everywhere ought to enjoy and all our moral influence should be exerted to secure them for all mankind.

—ROBERT E. SPEER,
Ex-President, Federal Council of the Churches of Christ in America

The Basis For Unity

THE BILL OF RIGHTS is a foundation of our democracy but it is too often interpreted in a way that promotes intolerance. It must be realized that the rights for which it stands carry with them an obligation not only to recognize the rights of others but to listen with sympathy and understanding when others exercise those rights. In other words, it is an interpretation of the basis of democracy, the unique importance of individual personality. Only by the weaving together of differing talents do we achieve unity.

—CHARLES P. TAFT,
*Assistant Director of Defense Health
and Welfare Services,
Federal Security Agency*

An Ever Living Legacy

TO ME, THE BILL OF RIGHTS symbolizes the essence of democracy, both as a form of government for the nation and as a "way of life" for the people. Although adopted as an Amendment, the Bill of Rights is the very heart of the Constitution.

The Bill of Rights is a guarantee in perpetuity of the inalienable right of every citizen to "life, liberty, and the pursuit of happiness." It is America's basic charter of human freedom. It makes the Declaration of Independence and the Constitution an ever living legacy of liberty.

Today, as never before in our history, the Bill of Rights is challenged—not by internal enemies but by foreign totalitarian forces. If human freedom is to be preserved, Americans must value their historic heritage more than life itself.

Wendell Willkie said in San Francisco on July 24, 1940: "Only men willing, if need be, to die for freedom, will have freedom." The spirit of Patrick Henry must live again in the hearts of all who love liberty.

The United States is the "last best hope of earth" in saving democracy and building a world-ordered society of free men. The time has come when America must keep a momentous "rendezvous with destiny."

It may be that Americans again must die for liberty. Whatever the cost, democracy, as a way of life and as a form of government, must be preserved—for ourselves and for our posterity.

—E. Guy Talbott,
Field Secretary, World Alliance
for International Friendship
Through the Churches

The Final Victory

THE FOUNDING FATHERS established "a more perfect Union," to make effective the majority will by democratic and orderly means. But into the self-same Constitution the people wrote a Bill of Rights, recognizing that the ultimate test of government for as well as by themselves is the fullest enjoyment by every person of freedom of speech, press, assembly and religion. "The general voice of America," as Jefferson described the popular will, demanded and obtained this added security for liberty.

These written constitutional guaranties have provided a check on occasional attempts at official tyranny; but that is not the key to their survival. Abroad, one European nation after another has lost its freedom, in the face of solemn pronouncements in its fundamental law. At home, civil liberties have been infringed by popular passion and prejudice far more frequently than by the calculated action of Congress, the Executive or the Courts. The fact is that our heritage of individual liberty has survived because we as a people have cherished and generally practiced it in our daily lives, and because we as a nation have defended it by arms against every external foe.

From earliest days, our population has been made up of immigrants and the sons of immigrants, of a multitude of racial, religious and cultural backgrounds, all fleeing some form of oppression, all joined in a love of freedom. Under the protecting shield of individual liberty, each strain in our varied population has contributed its full share toward the common goal of national greatness. As the machine age opened up new problems and new tyrannies, we have broadened the responsibilities of government in the economic sphere, so that farmers and factory workers might be truly free. With every passing year, new blows for the rights of the underprivileged have been struck by Congress, the Courts, and an intelligent and alert public opinion. The crisis of the times has given new urgency to our efforts in meeting and overcoming long-suffered injustices and perfecting our democratic heritage.

Today, the maintenance of that heritage is as challenging as it was in the formative period one hundred and fifty years ago. What *we* do or fail to do is even more decisive for the future of the Bill of Rights than the historic words and deeds of the Founding Fathers.

In the warfare being waged by the Axis against democratic institutions everywhere, a bombardment of subversive ideas may be as potent as an attack with airplanes and tanks. The Nazi Minister of Enlightenment and Propaganda has proclaimed that "nothing will be easier than to produce a bloody revolution in North America. No other country has so many social and racial tensions. We shall be able to play on many strings there." A noisy handful of Dr. Goebbels' dupes and apologists have been injecting his shop-worn propaganda and his racial animosities into the currents of American debate on foreign policy. This abuse of the freedom sanctioned by the Bill of Rights must and will be answered by facts, not suppression. We know that democracy has not run its race; for our system has built here the world's highest standards of life, while the nations controlled by dictatorship sink deeper into starvation and despair. We know that Nazi racial dogmas will never win support in this free land; for our history of inter-racial cooperation and harmony is the perennial goal of suffering Europe, while Hitler's conception of a master race has earned universal hate and scorn. Above all, we know that the Bill of Rights springs from the humanity and religious heritage of all civilized men, while Nazism is a reversion to the pagan and barbaric.

On this fateful anniversary of the Bill of Rights, let us therefore proclaim that ours is the glory and the future. With God's help, ours will be the final victory.

—ROBERT F. WAGNER,
United States Senator

A Bill Of Duties

THE CHIEF VALUE of a commemorating celebration is to point the road to the future. We look back 150 years to the birth of the Bill of Rights. It is equally worthwhile to look forward 150 years and ask ourselves what we are doing now that will be worthy of commemoration then.

I can't help thinking that it is all-important for every citizen in the United States to reinforce the written Bill of Rights with an unwritten Bill of Duties engraved on his heart. There will never be in the United States a Nazi or Fascist overlord, telling each individual citizen just what his or her duty is. But in order to avoid this, it is vital that every citizen should think vigorously in his own way about his duty day by day to the general welfare. If this feeling is strong enough, the Bill of Rights will mean as much to our descendants 150 years from now as it does to us today.

—HENRY A. WALLACE,
Vice President of the United States

An Unimpaired Heritage

THE BILL OF RIGHTS is a covenant between the American people and their Government. It is a covenant which guarantees to the individual citizen the maintenance of civil liberties and the protection of human dignity and freedom against inroads by the State.

But unless the Bill of Rights is also interpreted as a Bill of Duties, this guarantee is unfulfillable.

In the last analysis, the Bill of Rights is a contract between each American citizen and his fellow citizens —a contract which requires that we fulfill our duties in order that we may enjoy our rights—a contract which requires that we neither abuse our rights nor trespass upon the similar rights of others.

No mere written document—not even our Constitution—can guarantee us the preservation of the freedoms for which our forefathers fought and died. Only our own eternal vigilance—only our own everlasting willingness to sacrifice, to fight and, if necessary, to die for the maintenance of our freedom, can insure our handing down to our children an unimpaired heritage of freedom and human dignity.

—JAMES P. WARBURG

The Essence Of Civilization

SO INGRAINED IN THE MIND and spirit of the American people is the philosophy of the Bill of Rights that until recently it seemed fantastic that it should ever be challenged.

The hideous barbarism of the Nazi revolution of reaction is the exact opposite of all the guarantees of the Bill of Rights. The Nazi-Fascist thesis is that the few should enslave and utilize the many and that freedom is dangerous whether it be freedom of action, speech, press, conscience or thought. The Nazi allegation is that a single Fuehrer should possess absolute power and that he and his henchmen are supermen.

Such was probably the idea of many of the petty tyrants and bandits against whom the liberty-loving men and women of the world dared to demand and succeeded in securing the Bill of Rights. The precious liberties they won are better appreciated now that we have seen in action the contrasting degradation which dictatorship seeks to impose.

The Bill of Rights is the declaration of the dignity of the individual as a member of a civilized community with the right to worship according to his conscience, the right to think freely, the opportunity to speak, print, write and do what he believes is proper, subject only to the obligations of respecting similar rights among his fellows.

The Bill of Rights embodies the relationship of the individual to society and of society to the individual. It has grown with the times but the sturdiness of its spirit was full-blown at its birth.

The essence of the Bill of Rights is our tolerance of the same reasonable liberties in others which we believe proper for ourselves and our defense of our own liberties against encroachment by anyone who would trespass beyond the bounds it imposes.

Today we must renew our fervent loyalty to these principles lest either complacency or prejudice rob us of the ennobling democracy which it breathes into a free nation. We who possess this doctrine of mutual decency must defend it from within or from without.

The Bill of Rights has been a beacon light leading mankind out of the darkness of barbarism and those who prattle that dictatorship is the wave of the future forget that dictatorship was the slough of the past and that democracy has led mankind out of the degradation of the past. The spirit of Christianity has led men out of slavery by inculcating the dignity and responsibility of the soul of man which have joined in making the Bill of Rights the essence of modern civilization. Let us, in our nation, keep marching ahead, holding firm the individual liberties and responsibilities of our Bill of Rights.

—ROBERT J. WATT,
International Representative,
American Federation of Labor

*To Celebrate Liberty

THE CELEBRATION of the Fourth of July distinctly is set to revive the glorious memory of the Declaration of Independence. For the principles of liberty which have given survival values to our American government, stem back to the Declaration of Independence. That Declaration was a fiery, revolutionary defy aimed at the powers of kings who ruled without the consent of the governed. That Declaration was a voice crying in the wilderness for the establishment of liberties that the world then did not understand. A few agitators, philosophers and visionaries were writing about the things embodied in our Declaration when it was published. But our demands for liberty roused the laughter of kings and were greeted with contempt by the ruling powers of the world. Yet all the freedom demanded by that revolutionary declaration later was embodied in the Constitution of the United States— not in the original draft but in the preamble and that part of the Constitution known as the Bill of Rights.

Our Constitution today and all its wise framework of government rests upon the guarantees of liberty embodied in that Bill of Rights.

It is to celebrate liberty that we have set aside this Fourth of July. Without liberty no guarantees of government are valid. Deny the liberties that are guaranteed to the American people by the Bill of Rights, liberties which came straight out of the impulse of the Declaration of Independence, and all the wise checks and balances set up in our Constitution will collapse and free government will pass in this nation.

If by some social or political cataclysm our Constitution itself should be abolished, and the preamble with the Bill of Rights might be left intact, the Constitution would be restored within a year. But if the Bill of Rights were wiped out and the Constitution only survived without the liberties of free speech, free conscience, free assemblage, a free press, the right of the writ of habeas corpus, and the trial by jury, then all the wise provisions of the Constitution itself soon would disappear. Never forget this: our country could survive any shock if our liberties remained. It could stand no social change if we lost our liberties. A constitutional government that is not upheld by free men would soon be a tyranny no matter how wisely the Constitution were framed, no matter how carefully it were worded.

So this day we celebrate America, the land of the free. Here is a country where men of every race and creed, men of every form of political belief, men of every aspiring dream for a better world, may have their say and go their peaceful ways. The Constitution embodies the rules for the orderly process of democracy. But the Constitution triumphs because and only because it is buttressed and backed up by the Bill of Rights which came out of the philosophy of the Declaration of Independence. The orderly constitutional processes of democracy hold their place and function as the foundation of our Republic buttressed by the loyal love of free men. For strong and firm as our constitutional foundation is today, let us remember that under the foundations of our government are the footing stones, those previous liberties of the individual which come through the Bill of Rights mortised in the Declaration of Independence celebrated this day. Our Constitution is the wisest document that man has ever penned. How quickly would it crumble into dust if the guarantees of freedom should go—those blessings of liberty which rose out of the Declaration of Independence and were written indelibly in the Bill of Rights.

So today we hail that Rebel Declaration of Independence! It is a charter of our liberties in this land of the free, this home of the brave—where to be brave we must be free, where the free must be ever brave.

—WILLIAM ALLEN WHITE

Substance of an address delivered by William Allen White over a coast to coast radio hook up on July 4th, under the auspices of the Council Against Intolerance in America.

Old Principles For New Situations

THE TEN AMENDMENTS to the Constitution which we call the Bill of Rights have a meaning as vital to Americans of today as to the Americans of 1791 who wrote them. The freedoms of worship, speech, press and assembly which American citizens guaranteed to themselves 150 years ago are the same freedoms this nation is determined to defend in 1941.

The Bill of Rights is the great charter of individual liberty and the dignity of the individual. As such it lies close to the hearts of farm men and women. Although farmers as a group claim no superiority over other groups of Americans in love of liberty and in patriotism, they surely come second to no other group. The United States of 1791 was an agrarian nation. Practically all the men who formed the Bill of Rights, who passed it in Congress, and who ratified it in State Legislatures were either farmers or men elected by farmers.

Farmers are as willing to work and fight for the Bill of Rights now as they were then; and they will fight for the spirit of the Bill of Rights, not just for the enshrined letter. In their striving for economic democracy farmers now are applying the old principles to new situations which have arisen. They are making farm programs work so that farmers can have a say in their own destiny.

For all American citizens, as well as for farmers, the first ten Amendments to the Constitution are the guarantee that the state will exist to serve the individual, not the individual to serve the state. We are prepared to guard that guarantee by force of arms against any threat from without. And by warring against poverty, disease and malnutrition which are the breeding ground of intolerance and race hatred, we are prepared also to meet threats from within.

—CLAUDE R. WICKARD,
United States Secretary of Agriculture

Never More Precious

THOUGH IT SOUND TRITE to speak of the supreme significance of the Bill of Rights, never was it more need-
ful to remember that it is just another link in the
chain which stretches from the Magna Charta of
Runnymede in 1215 to the Declaration of Independence of Philadelphia in 1776. The highly spiritual
promises of the Constitution secured their ultimate
guarantees through the Bill of Rights which was
prophecy of what a democracy must come to be.

The Bill of Rights is more precious than ever before
because of the momentary—it cannot be permanent—
abrogation of parallel ideas first proclaimed in the
same year, 1789, in and by the French Republic and
because of the unashamed attack of totalitarianism
everywhere upon those institutions of democracy
which have waxed mighty under the aegis or inspira-
tion of the American Bill of Rights!

For the first time in our history, the Bill of Rights
is threatened from without. For a Hitler-conquered
and Hitler-ruled world would mean the abrogation of
the Bill of Rights, the cancellation of democracy, the
enslavement of men. To keep the Bill of Rights inviolate, let us in this sesqui-centennial of its adoption
dedicate our lives, our fortunes, and our sacred honor.

—STEPHEN S. WISE,
President, American Jewish Congress

The Breath Of Life

WHAT DOES THE BILL OF RIGHTS mean to me? It means the very breath of life!

Perhaps it took the vicious attack of the Nazi regime upon the rights of the individual to bring us to a realization of their meaning. We had taken too much for granted; given as little thought to the freedom which we enjoy as to the air which we breathe.

Now that freedom is threatened it is time for each one of us to rally to its defense; to guard the inalienable rights of every human being to freedom of worship, of speech, of the press, of assembly, of petition.

No one of our possessions is comparable to the ideals of liberty, tolerance and equality upon which this Republic was founded. May we, too, be willing to pledge for their maintenance "our lives, our fortunes and our sacred honor."

—MARY E. WOOLLEY,
President Emeritus, Mt. Holyoke College

INDEX OF CONTRIBUTORS

INDEX OF CONTRIBUTORS